from Palette to Palate

CULINARY ARTWORKS FROM THE DIGBY PINES KITCHEN

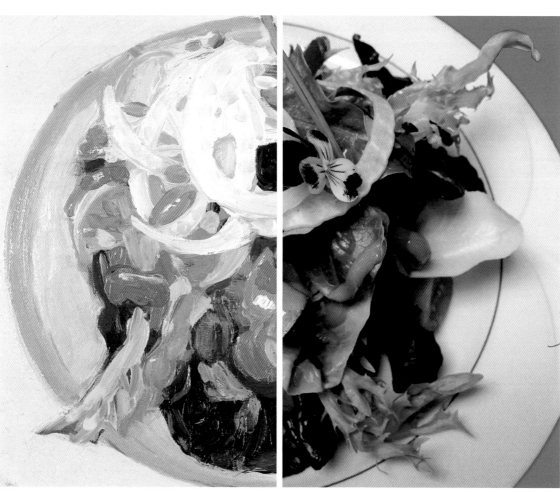

June 24, 2022
TMAC Dine Around
at the Digby Pines.

Chef Dale Nichols

Artist Lynda Shalagan / *Chef* Dale Nichols

SSP Publications

SSP Publications recognizes the support of the Province of Nova Scotia. We are pleased to work in partnership with the Department of Communities, Culture and Heritage to develop and promote our cultural resources for all Nova Scotians.

Library and Archives Canada Cataloguing in Publication

Nichols, Dale, 1957-, author
    From palette to palate : culinary works from the Digby
Pines' kitchen / Chef Dale Nichols ; artist , Lynda Shalagan.

Includes index.
ISBN 978-0-9868733-7-9 (softcover)

    1. Cooking, Canadian—Maritime Provinces style. 2. Cooking—
Nova Scotia—Digby. 3. Digby Pines Golf Resort and Spa (Digby, N.S.).
4. Cookbooks. I. Shalagan, Lynda, illustrator II. Title.

TX715.6.N533 2018   641.59716'32   C2018-901365-6

Design: Co. & Co.
Printed in Canada
All food photos by Dale Nichols
All photos of Lynda Shalagan's paintings by Eric Boutilier-Brown

Box 2472, Halifax, NS, B3J 3E4 Canada
www.sspub.ca
sspub@hotmail.com

"Palette to Palate connects The Pines' culinary creativity with the art world.

We are proud to display our local products on canvas in a marriage of Dale's fresh food approach with Lynda's artistic interpretations"

— Rene Leblanc
    GM, Digby Pines Golf Resort and Spa

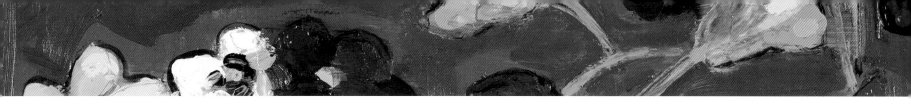

INTRODUCTIONS

Dale Nichols

When I became a chef, it was never my intention to write a cookbook. I watched as some of my chef associates produced wonderful works of their culinary excellence. I actually bought a few for my own collection, but the bug wasn't there yet to make an effort of my own.

Nova Scotia is the best kept culinary secret in the country. I am fortunate enough to have a growing pool of local producers delivering fresh product right to our back door of The Pines. Fortunate enough to be able to create our 100km Special, which is our environmental initiative where everything on this plate comes from within a 100 km radius of the Digby Pines. The 100km Special is an evolving plate in that, as local produce comes out of the ground, we can introduce it to our plates. This is every chef's dream — tasting produce that, an hour earlier, was still on the vine or attached to a tree! I would be remiss if I didn't mention our grounds team, led by Kasha, who have built us a beautiful herb garden right outside the kitchen door. We grow sage, chives, tarragon, oregano, dill, beebalm, edible flowers and several kinds of thyme. It is a great place to meet guests of the hotel while we pick herbs and flowers for our evening service.

So here I am, working on a cookbook of the culinary artwork our Pines kitchen team has produced over the past nine years. Where to begin?

I want to pass some of this passion on to the readers of this book and if they attempt to make these creations, I have tried to break down the recipes to their simplest form so that the typical home cook can prepare them. I have tried to envision every step the home cook may encounter to be able to recreate these dishes. Some are long preparations, but the final results are worth it. ENJOY !!

Lynda Shalagan

To arrange and paint the bounty of nature in a still life has always been exciting to me from my first painting forages in art school. I spent many years visiting the Halifax Farmer's Market bringing home armfuls of the fresh, colourful, local produce to paint... and eventually to eat. To be able to include such images alongside the artistry of the recipes of Chef Dale Nichols feels very satisfying. The simple beauty of the individual ingredients transformed and put onto the plate create another level of visual beauty in the hands of Chef Nichols... and then there is the taste!

ACKNOWLEDGEMENTS

There have been many people who have supported me over the years. Too many to be able to mention here, but I would be remiss if I did not mention my fellow Digby Pines managers, especially our General Manager Rene Leblanc, who has always allowed me creative license with our menus. Their encouragement and critiques are appreciated in order to give our guests as great a culinary experience as possible. Then there are the cooks, especially our Sous Chef Reinier Boermans, who has given me his full support for nine years. I thank all who have passed through The Pines kitchen and who have slugged it out with me year after year, where amidst all the craziness, we manage to have a little fun. Bravo to them for helping create and put these dishes to the plate.

—*Dale Nichols*

DEDICATIONS

Early in my career, a wise man told me, "We work while everyone else is having fun". In this occupation, no truer words can be spoken. I have been lucky in my career, and I was lucky enough to find the perfect life mate, Pat, who for thirty plus years has understood, and endured, life with a chef.

This cookbook is dedicated to Pat and my daughter Kelly, who have backed me all the way in my career. Christmases have been derailed, birthdays celebrated later, Pat and Kelly going solo to family and social gatherings — but never any pushback to what I do and the time commitment it involves. I will be forever grateful.

—*Dale Nichols*

I would like to dedicate this book and offer my continuing support to all the organic farmers in the Maritimes who are committed to providing healthy options for our dinner table.

— *Lynda Shalagan*

FOREWORD

Growing up just outside Annapolis Royal, I had the privilege of being raised by parents, who as artists embraced creativity in all of its forms. Our home was a canvas where writing on our bedroom walls was not only encouraged but occasionally critiqued. My father's studio was originally housed in our basement and all viable wall space exploded with large colorful works that demanded their viewer look beyond the obvious. This home became a constant source of inspiration and shaped my belief that art can truly be found in all we see, hear, feel and taste.

As a child I remember The Digby Pines as an enigma, an elegant castle on the hill steeped in history and prestige. It wasn't until later in life that I realized that property could become part of my own story. After several false starts and tireless self-analysis, a rather simplified theme emerged...I was fascinated by people, I enjoyed beauty in all forms, and I was fiercely proud of the area in which I was raised. Keeping in line with my love of the finer things in life, The imposing Norman Style Castle overlooking the tides of the Annapolis Basin, with its manicured gardens and European aesthetics would be where I would set my sights. And so began my nearly 20-year long love affair with The Digby Pines Hotel.

I first met Chef Dale Nichols in 2003 while on recruiting trips around Atlantic Canada, and I had only recently embarked on my career in the hospitality industry. Although, both excited and nervous to be working alongside seasoned professionals, I was able to witness his commitment to the craft and respect he held for his recruits and the industry. Chef Dale would officially join our team at the Digby Pines in 2007. He quickly became an integral part of our operation and moreover, a friend. Never one to shy away from a challenge and always searching for new ways to express himself, he proved to be an artist in his own right. Beyond his talent in the kitchen and passion for his craft, he is a true mentor who leads with dedication, humor and comradery on both sides of the swinging kitchen doors.

Chef Dale aspires for his culinary offerings to compete with the best in the world and excels at designing menus that support the abundant resources our area and its producers have to offer. His dishes are as aesthetically pleasing as they are delicious and are often creatively titled. They inspire stories to be shared of, not only their origins, but of the relationships he has built with area farmers, artisan growers, fishermen and his own culinary team. A cookbook with recipes as inspired as the artwork it accompanies certainly lives up to the title, *From Palette to Palate*.

Annah Boucher
Director of Operations
Digby Pines Golf Resort and Spa

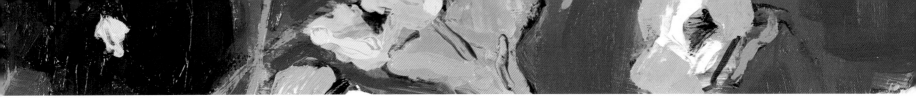

CONTENTS

GARDEN FRESH

Wild Rose Certified Organic Salad

APPLE CIDER VINAIGRETTE, SIMPSON ELITE,
RED AND GREEN OAK, SNOW PEA SHOOTS,
LOLLA ROSSA, ARUGULA, RED SAILS

Wild Rose Farms is located about 25 km from the Digby Pines.
Gilberte Doel is a passionate certified organic farmer and, in these
times of healthy diets and knowing where our food comes from,
I am happy to feature her products on our menus each year.

Serves 8 or more

NOTE ON INGREDIENTS

If you don't live in the Annapolis Digby area, visit your local farmers' market
and search for certified organics. They are more plentiful and with more
variety each year. Similar to salad greens, goat cheese is also a locally
produced cheese available at local markets. If you are not an Atlantic
Canadian, support your local outdoor farmers markets and use the great
products they grow. Hear their stories and create a relationship. They will
never let you down.

To wrap in rice paper, drag the rice paper through cold water and lay it on
a cutting board. It will soften as the water absorbs. Arrange some lettuce
leaves in the same direction. Centre them on the rice paper and roll the
rice paper, leaving the ends of the lettuce revealed. Arrange on a plate
and garnish with the goat cheese, vinaigrette and perhaps a few of your
favourite berries.

APPLE CIDER VINAIGRETTE

- 2 **cups local apple cider**
- 1 **tbsp Dijon mustard**
- 4 **drops tabasco sauce**
- 4 **drops Worcestershire sauce**
- 2 **tbsp apple cider vinegar**
- 3 **cups virgin olive oil**
  Salt and pepper

Bring the apple cider to a boil and reduce by half. Cool and chill in a stainless
steel bowl. Add the remainder of the ingredients except the oil. Using a wire
whisk, vigorously whisk in the canola oil. Season with salt and pepper.

TIP: Test your vinaigrettes for strength and flavor with a piece of lettuce
or a small chunk of bread.

Churchill's Seasonal Green Salad

FENNEL JULIENNE, GRILLED PEPPERS, TOMATOES,
MAPLE GINGER VINAIGRETTE

Supermarkets carry every different lettuce variety available these days.
The cultural diversities make that a necessity for them. Small containers
of artisan lettuces are available to use in this plate.

Serves 8

4　heads of miniature artisan lettuces like red oak, green oak, frisee, mini green leaf – trim the butt end and break the heads of lettuce apart and wash well

1　head Belgian endive – trim the core and break off the leaves whole

1　head fennel – shaved ⅛ inch thick across the bulb to give thin julienne affect

1　red pepper – cut in half, seeds and stem removed

1　yellow pepper – cut in half, seeds and stem removed

16　red grape tomatoes – cut in quarters (use other colours if you wish)
　　Maple Ginger Vinaigrette

Cut each half of the peppers into three sections. Toss the sections with a little canola oil and season with salt and pepper. On a hot BBQ or a home kitchen grill, mark the peppers well and immediately put them into the refrigerator or a place to cool them quickly. When cool, cut them into strips as thin as you like.

Spoon a little dressing onto each plate. Arrange a few whole pieces of the lettuces onto the plates. Insert some pieces of the red and yellow peppers and the grape tomato quarters. Top with some of the shaved fennel and dress with some more of the maple ginger vinaigrette.

MAPLE GINGER VINAIGRETTE

1　garlic clove

1　medium shallot

1　inch piece fresh ginger root – peeled and chopped

2　tbsp Dijon mustard

2　tbsp maple syrup

3　tbsp balsamic vinegar

½　cup olive oil

½　cup canola oil
　　Salt and black pepper

In a blender, or food processor, combine the garlic, shallot, ginger, mustard, soy sauce, maple syrup, and balsamic vinegar until liquified. With the motor running on low, gradually add the olive oil and canola oil. Season with salt and black pepper.

Baby Spinach Salad with Cardamom Poached Pears

SPICED PECANS, CANADIAN CAMEMBERT CHEESE, SHERRY VINEGAR DRESSING

Serves 8

16 oz baby spinach

8 oz Camembert cheese – cut in long 1 oz spears

Spiced Pecans

Cardamom Pears

Sherry Maple Lime Vinaigrette

Arrange the baby spinach in the center of each plate. Slice the pear halves in thin slices, still attached at the top and fan them slightly against the spinach. Lean the spear of camembert against pear. Dress over and around the salad with the sherry vinaigrette and garnish with several of the spiced pecans.

SPICED PECANS

1 egg white

2 cups pecans

½ tsp cinnamon

1 tsp icing sugar

Preheat oven to 250°F.

Whisk the egg white to a broken bubbly froth. Add the pecans, cinnamon and icing sugar. Bake in the oven for 45 minutes, turning after 25 minutes.

Let cool. Pecans will be soft immediately from the oven, but will crisp as they cool.

POACHING SYRUP FOR CARDAMOM PEARS

4 cups water

1 cup brown sugar

1 cup white wine

Juice from one lemon

2 tbsp ground cardamom

6 pieces whole clove

4 pears – slightly under-ripe

Peel and half the pears, and remove the core and stems. Bring everything else to a boil to dissolve the sugar. Turn to medium heat. Add the pears. Cook until pears are soft to the center. Cool for later.

TIP: Place a piece of parchment or wax paper over the pears to hold them beneath the surface of the syrup, or pears may float and not cook evenly.

SHERRY MAPLE LIME VINAIGRETTE

1 tbsp shallots – finely chopped

6 drops Worcestershire sauce

6 drops tabasco sauce

1 tbsp Dijon mustard

1 oz sherry vinegar

½ oz lime juice

2 tsp red wine vinegar

2 tbsp maple syrup

1 cup mayonnaise

Salt and pepper

Whisk together everything except the mayonnaise, salt and pepper. Add the mayonnaise, whisk well and season to taste with the salt and pepper.

Non-Traditional Caesar Salad wrapped in Rice Paper

SHAVED PARMESAN, BACON CRISPS, OLIVE OIL
CROUTONS, OVEN DRIED TOMATOES, ROASTED GARLIC

Every restaurant has a Caesar Salad that is unique to them.
Guests will order the Caesar Salad everywhere they go, to be able
to compare, and decide which one is their favorite.

Serves 8

2 heads romaine lettuce

8 large rice papers

16 bacon rashers – baked in the oven to render the fat and make crisp bacon

8 oz shaved parmesan

2 cups olive oil croutons

24 pcs Oven Dried Grape Tomatoes

½ cup Quick Roasted Garlic (see Recipe Appendix page 123)

2 cups Caesar Dressing

Cut the butt off the lettuce and trim any brown edges. Halve lengthwise. Cut the two halves of romaine in long strips about ½ to ¾ inch wide.

To wrap the romaine in rice paper, drag the rice paper through cold water and lay it on a cutting board. It will soften as the water absorbs. Arrange a large handful of romaine lettuce leaves in the same direction in the centre of the rice paper. Centre them on the rice paper and lift the front part of the rice paper over the romaine and tuck it back in against the romaine. Roll the rice paper slightly, fold the ends in, and finish the roll. The sticky of the rice paper will help glue the roll together.

On each plate, drag some Caesar dressing around in a random pattern. Cut a small portion off the end of the rice paper. Make two more cuts in the roll to create three equal portions. Arrange the portions on the plate, open side up, and repeat for the rest of the plates. Spoon some additional Caesar dressing into the open ends of the rice paper rolls.

Garnish the plates with two bacon rashers broken into smaller pieces. Place croutons on and around the rice paper rolls. Add three dried tomatoes to each plate and a few pieces of roasted garlic. Finish by placing an ounce of shaved parmesan over top of the rice paper rolls.

OVEN DRIED TOMATOES

4 cups grape tomatoes

2 tbsp canola oil

1 tbsp dried basil

Preheat oven to 150°F.

Toss the tomatoes in the canola oil and dried basil. Place on a baking sheet and place in the oven overnight, approximately 10 hours. Remove from oven and cool until ready to use.

OLIVE OIL CROUTONS

1 lb slab of focaccia bread

4 oz extra virgin olive oil

2 tbsp mixed dried herbs – thyme, oregano, basil, marjoram

Salt and pepper

Preheat oven to 350°F.

Cut the focaccia into small cubes and toss with the olive oil, herbs, salt and pepper. Spread croutons out on a sheet pan and bake for 15 to 20 minutes, stirring often. Bake until the croutons begin to brown around the edges but remain soft in the center.

CAESAR DRESSING

- 2 tbsp Dijon mustard
- 2 tbsp garlic – chopped
- 3 tsp cracked black pepper
- 2 tbsp anchovy paste
- 2 tbsp lemon juice
- 2 tbsp red wine vinegar
- 4 tsp Worcestershire sauce
- 2 tsp tabasco sauce
- 2 cups mayonnaise
- 1 cup parmesan cheese
- ¼ cup olive oil

In a food processor, add all the ingredients except the mayonnaise, cheese and olive oil.

Pulse until well blended. Add in the mayonnaise and cheese and blend until well incorporated.

While the processor is running, slowly pour in the olive oil.

QUICK ROASTED GARLIC
See Recipe Appendix page 123

Roasted Beets, Endive, Radicchio and Arugula Salad

RANCHER GOAT CHEESE, CANDIED WALNUTS, ORANGE GASTRIQUE

One of the most popular salads we have ever produced. Guests love the combinations of the beets, goat cheese with the crunchy candied walnuts. Very fresh, very crisp.....it's ALIVE !!

Serves 8

8 medium sized purple beets, or multicolored beets if available
2 heads of Belgian endive
1 head of radicchio
4 cups baby arugula
12 oz Rancher goat cheese (1½ oz per salad)
1 cup Candied Walnuts
½ cup Orange Gastrique

ROASTING BEETS: Set the oven to 350°F. Remove the butt end and the pointed end of the beets. Toss the beets in some canola oil with salt and pepper. Wrap the beets in tin foil to create and oven with-in an oven and bake them for 1½ to 2 hours. Bake until soft to the center. Remove the beets from the oven, unwrap, and let them begin to cool. While they are warm take a cloth and begin to rub the beet, and the skins will come off leaving you with a nice shiny whole beet.

ASSEMBLE THE SALAD: Arrange the endive, radicchio and arugula in the center of the plate. Try to play architect and pile it up a bit. Slice one of the beets and arrange it on the salad. Sprinkle around the salad with the goat cheese and walnuts. Dress the salad with the orange gastrique.

ORANGE GASTRIQUE

1 cup sugar
½ cup rice wine vinegar
   Juice of 2 medium oranges
¼ cup blood orange purée
½ piece star anise
½ tsp cardamom

Tie the star anise and cardamom into a spice bag. Bring all ingredients to a boil. Reduce by ¾ or until mix has thickened like a syrup.

CANDIED WALNUTS

2 egg whites
4 cups walnuts
1 tsp cinnamon
2 tsp icing sugar

Preheat oven to 250°F.

Whisk the egg whites to a broken bubbly froth. Add the walnuts, cinnamon and icing sugar.

Bake in the oven for 1 hour, turning after 30 minutes. Cool and serve.

TIP: Walnuts will be soft immediately from the oven, but will crisp as they cool

Grilled Vegetable Salad

ASIAGO CHEESE, ISRAELI COUSCOUS, RED ONION,
BALSAMIC HONEY REDUCTION, EXTRA VIRGIN
OLIVE OIL

Serves 8

4 oz Asiago cheese – shaved into petals
8 small handfulls of salad greens like arugula, mizuna, lolla rossa or oak leaf
  Grilled Vegetables
  Israeli Couscous
  Balsamic Honey Reduction

Arrange some of the grilled vegetables criss-cross onto each plate. Place a small handful of greens on top of the vegetables. Sprinkle a generous amount of the Israeli couscous over and around the salad and vegetables. Spoon some shaved asiago cheese over top and drizzle balsamic honey reduction on and around the salad. Finish with some good quality extra virgin olive oil.

GRILLED VEGETABLES

4 medium size carrots – peeled
4 medium zucchini
2 red peppers – cut in half, seed core and stem removed
2 yellow peppers – cut in half, seed core and stem removed
1 large red onion – peeled and sliced in ¼ inch rings
1 oz canola oil
  Salt and pepper

Turn on your BBQ or kitchen grill to high.

Cut the carrots ¼ inch thick planks lengthwise and blanch briefly, then cool.

Cut the zucchini ¼ inch thick planks lengthwise.

Cut the pepper halves in three pieces.

In a large stainless steel bowl, toss all of the vegetables with the canola oil and season with salt and pepper. Grill all of the vegetables and cool them immediately in the fridge to retain their crispness.

ISRAELI COUSCOUS

2 tsp olive oil
1 garlic clove – minced
½ small onion – finely chopped
1½ cups Israeli couscous
1½ cups vegetable broth
1 cup water

Heat the olive oil in a small saucepan over medium high heat. Add garlic and onion, saute until the onion is translucent and starting to brown. Add couscous and stir, cooking for one minute. Add broth and water, place the lid on and turn the heat down to medium low. Cook for 10 minutes until the liquid is absorbed and the couscous is cooked through but still firm. Use a fork to separate the couscous and transfer to a bowl to cool.

BALSAMIC HONEY REDUCTION

1 cup brown sugar
1 cup Ridgeview honey
6 cups balsamic vinegar

Add the ingredients to a large pot and bring to a boil.

Turn the heat down to medium low and reduce until the mixture can coat the back of a spoon and seems thick when rubbed between the fingers.

Strawberry and Mango Salad

ARUGULA, TOASTED PINE NUTS, RED ONION,
ORANGE INFUSED QUINOA, BALSAMIC REDUCTION,
EXTRA VIRGIN OLIVE OIL

Serves 8

2 mangos – peeled, sides cut off, and cut in long thin strips

16 strawberries – stem removed and cut in very thin slices

½ cup pine nuts – toasted

4 cups arugula

½ oz canola oil

1 large red onion – cut in ¼ inch wide rings

¼ cup red wine vinegar

¼ cup honey

½ tsp ground cardamom

  Salt and pepper

  Orange Infused Quinoa

  Balsamic Reduction

CANDIED RED ONION: In a medium fry pan, add the oil and saute the red onion briefly. Add the red wine vinegar. The onions will turn a brighter red. Cook one minute and add the honey and cardamom. Allow the onions to soften and remove from the pan to a small bowl. Reduce the honey and cardamom to a thick syrup and pour over the onions. Refrigerate to cool.

Portion some of the quinoa on each plate. Stand the strawberries straight up on the plate and push slices apart like a fan. Arrange mango strips. Divide the arugula on the plates and the candied red onion. Drizzle with the balsamic reduction and some extra virgin olive oil. Sprinkle with pine nuts and serve.

ORANGE INFUSED QUINOA

2 tsp olive oil

½ medium onion – chopped fine

1 cup orange juice

½ tsp salt

1 cup quinoa

  Zest of 1 orange – chopped fine

½ cup dried black currents

½ cup parsley - chopped

In a medium saucepan, heat oil over medium heat. Add onion and cook until soft.

Add orange juice, 1 cup water and salt. Bring to a boil. Reduce heat to low, cover and simmer 15 to 20 minutes, until water is absorbed and quinoa is tender. Add in the orange zest. Remove from heat and let stand 3 minutes. Stir in the black currents and parsley.

BALSAMIC REDUCTION

2 cups balsamic vinegar

1 cup brown sugar

Combine in a sauce pan and reduce until the reduction thickens and becomes very shiny. The reduction will develop thick bubbles on the surface as it reduces. Drizzle over top of the salad.

Wild Mushroom Lasagna

WILD MUSHROOMS, ASPARAGUS, SPINACH, OKA CHEESE, BUTTERNUT SQUASH PURÉE

The key to this recipe is frying the mushrooms to achieve great flavour to carry through the lasagna.
The nutty Oka cheese creates an earthy flavour that works great with the silky butternut squash purée.

Serves 10 - 12

MUSHROOM LASAGNA

Salt – for water; extra as needed

Canola oil

12 **lasagna noodles**

4 **cups whole milk**

12 **tbsp unsalted butter**

½ **cup app-purpose flour**

1 **tsp ground black pepper**

1½ **lbs field mushrooms, cremini mushrooms and portobello mushrooms**

2 **tbsp mix of dried basil and oregano**

½ **lb Oka cheese or raclette cheese**

1 **lb grated mozzarella cheese**

1 **lb baby spinach – steamed and squeezed**

FOR SERVING

30 **asparagus spears cut in 5 inch lengths and quickly blanched**

Butternut Squash Purée

Preheat oven to 350°F.

Bring a large pot of water to a boil with 1 tablespoon of salt and a small amount of oil. Add the lasagna noodles and cook for 10 minutes, stirring occasionally. Drain and set aside.

For the white sauce, bring the milk to a simmer in a saucepan. Set aside. Melt 8 tablespoons of the butter in a large saucepan. Add the flour and cook for 1 minute over low heat, stirring constantly with a wooden spoon. Pour the hot milk into the butter/flour mixture all at once. Add 1 tsp of salt, the pepper, and nutmeg, and cook over medium-low heat, stirring first with the wooden spoon and then with a whisk, for 3 to 4 minutes until thick. Set aside off the heat.

Slice the mushrooms. Heat 2 tbsp of oil and 2 tbsp of the butter in a large saucepan. When the butter melts, add half the mushrooms, sprinkle with salt, and cook over medium heat for about 5 minutes, until the mushrooms are tender and they release some of their juices. Add half the basil and oregano. If they become too dry, add a little more oil. Toss occasionally to make sure the mushrooms cook evenly. Repeat with the remaining mushrooms and set all the mushrooms aside. With a coarse grater, grate together the Oka and mozzarella cheese. Set aside.

To assemble the lasagna, spread some of the sauce in the bottom of an 8 × 12 × 2 inch glass baking dish. Arrange a layer of the noodles on top, then more sauce, then ⅓ of the mushrooms and a ¼ of the cheese. Distribute the spinach alternately between the layers. Repeat two more times, layering noodles, sauce, spinach, mushrooms and cheese. Top with a final layer of noodles and sauce, and sprinkle with the remaining cheese.

Bake the lasagna for 45 minutes to 1 hour until hot through and the top is brown.

Place a portion of lasagna in the center of the plate and spoon some of the butternut squash sauce over top. In a fry pan, warm the asparagus in a little butter and place over top of the lasagna

BUTTERNUT SQUASH PURÉE

1 **large butternut squash –
cut in half and seeds removed,
but leave skin on**

2 **tsp cinnamon**

½ **tsp allspice**

¼ **cup brown sugar**

1 **tbsp vanilla extract**

Salt and pepper

Preheat oven to 350°F.

Rub the flesh side of the squash with a small amount of cinnamon, allspice and brown sugar. Lay on a baking sheet, flesh side down and bake until the squash is ready to collapse and is very soft. Scoop the squash out of the skin and purée in a blender with a small amount of vanilla, salt and pepper. If the squash purée seems too thick, thin it out with a little vegetable stock or water.

Carrot Orange Ginger Soup

We prepare this carrot orange ginger soup for guests with eating sensitivities and for those lucky enough to have none. It fits all the options of vegan, vegetarian, gluten free, lactose intolerant and all major protein allergies. It is also very popular with our bus tours who frequent The Pines.

Serves 8 — 10

1 cup butter or canola oil (if preparing vegan)
2 medium onions – course chopped
2 lbs carrots – peeled and course chopped
½ cup fresh ginger – peeled and coarse chopped
4 cups orange juice – fairly good quality
2 cups vegetable stock (or water if necessary)
   Salt and pepper

In a medium stock pot, on medium heat, heat the canola oil and add the onions. Cook the onions until translucent, about 6 to 7 minutes. Add the carrots and ginger and cook until the carrots begin to soften. Season lightly with salt and pepper.

Add the orange juice and vegetable stock. Bring the soup to a boil and cook until the carrots are soft. Taste and adjust seasoning with salt and pepper along the way. Purée the soup in a blender until smooth. Return to a new pot, bring to a boil adjust seasoning and serve.

TIP: This soup can be served with a swirl of whipped cream and a toasted olive oil crouton

Leek and Butternut Squash Polenta

COCONUT LIME TOFU, WILD MUSHROOMS, ASPARAGUS, CHERRY APPLE ALMOND CHUTNEY, LEMON BUTTER SAUCE

This is a great vegetarian and gluten free dish that is a little different. With some notice, it can also be adapted to be a vegan meal as well.

Serves 8

8 squares Leek and Butternut Squash Polenta (3 × 3 inch) – pan fried to golden brown

24 asparagus spears – blanched and tossed in butter

2 cups cremini mushrooms – sautéed in butter, salt and pepper

8 slices Coconut Lime Tofu

8 large tbsp Cherry Apple Almond Chutney (see Recipe Appendix page 121)

Place the warm polenta cake in the center of the plate and place two or three asparagus spears on top. Scatter some of the cremini mushrooms on the asparagus and cover with a slice of the fried tofu. Spoon the chutney on top of the tofu. If you wish, finish the plate with a little drizzle of butter sauce, or even some warm extra virgin olive oil.

COCONUT LIME TOFU

1 can coconut milk

Juice from 2 limes

Zest from 1 lime

8 ½ inch thick slices of plain tofu

Salt and pepper

Mix together the coconut milk, lime juice and lime zest. Add in the tofu slices and let sit until ready to use. Season the tofu with salt and pepper and pan fry to put a little color on the tofu.

CHERRY APPLE ALMOND CHUTNEY

See Recipe Appendix page 121

BUTTERNUT SQUASH PURÉE

for polenta

1 whole butternut squash

2–4 tbsp maple syrup

¼ lb butter

Salt and white pepper

Preheat oven to 350°F.

Cut the butternut squash in half and scoop out the membranes with a spoon. Place halves face down on a baking sheet and pour a cup of water into the sheet pan. Bake for 30 to 40 minutes, or until the squash is fork tender. Remove from the oven.

Add the butter to a stainless-steel bowl. Spoon out the butternut squash and discard the peel.

Add the maple syrup. With a potato masher, mash the squash until the large chunks are gone. Season with salt and pepper. Place this mixture into a blender or food processor and purée. Adjust seasoning.

LEEK AND BUTTERNUT SQUASH POLENTA

¼ cup canola oil

1 cup white onion – chopped fine

1 cup leeks – white and light green end chopped fine

1½ cups butternut squash purée

4½ cups whole milk

1½ tsp salt

¼ tsp pepper

2 cups fine yellow cornmeal

3 egg yolks

1 cup parmesan cheese – grated

Heat the canola oil in a medium sauce pan over medium heat. Add the onions and leek and saute, stirring frequently until translucent, 5 to 6 minutes. Add the squash purée, milk, salt and pepper and bring to a boil. Reduce the heat to medium and slowly add the cornmeal in a thin stream while whisking continuously. Reduce the heat to low and simmer, stirring frequently with a whisk for about 5 minutes. The polenta will gather in the whisk without dripping out when it is ready. Remove the polenta from the heat and whisk in the egg yolks and parmesan cheese. Working quickly, spread the polenta onto a baking sheet and spread out to set and cool.

TIP: It is important to let the cornmeal cook out in order to set the polenta.

When the polenta is cooled and set, cut it into manageable squares and pan fry in a little butter to brown the polenta.

Grilled Mushroom Pizza

PESTO, LOCAL MOZZARELLA CHEESE, PEPPERS,
GRILLED ASPARAGUS, ASIAGO CHEESE

Pizza is the pie you happily learn how to eat. Experiment with different toppings in combination with different cheeses. If it all works, it's on to the next exciting combo.

For One Pizza

- 2 oz extra virgin olive oil
- 3 tbsp pesto
- ¾ cup grated mozzarella cheese
- ½ cup grated asiago cheese
- ½ cup cremini mushroom – sliced
- ½ cup shiitake mushrooms – sliced
- ½ cup oyster mushrooms – torn in small strips
- ½ cup grilled peppers – grilled ahead of time, cooled and cut in strips
- 5 asparagus spears – blanched, seasoned and grilled quickly. Chill and cut in 1 inch pieces.

Fry the mushrooms ahead of time in a small amount of butter and oil and set aside to cool.

Set oven to 425°F. If you have a pizza stone, put it in the oven now.

Roll out the pizza dough to the right size. Brush the dough with olive oil and flip the dough out onto the grill. When there are good grill marks on one side, flip the dough and mark the other side. Remove the dough to a pizza pan and begin adding the toppings.

Brush the pizza with a little more olive oil. Spread the pesto around the dough to create the back drop. Evenly sprinkle the mozzaerlla cheese over the pesto. Scatter the grilled peppers and asparagus to evenly cover the pizza. Finish with the asiago cheese and drizzle a little more olive oil on the pizza.

Lay the pizza directly on the pizza stone and bake for 3 minutes and check for doneness. The top and edges will be nicely browned and the bottom of the crust will feel dry to the touch. If not ready, leave for one more minute.

Remove from the oven, let rest for one minute and cut in 8 equal pieces.

PIZZA DOUGH

Makes 4 – 6 dough balls

- 1 cup warm water
- 2 tbsp active dry yeast
- 1 tbsp sugar
- 4 cups all purpose flour
- 2 tsp salt
- 2 tbsp extra virgin olive oil
- ¼ cup cornmeal

Dissolve the yeast in warm water. Add the flour, sugar and salt.

Add the olive oil. Knead in ¼ cup cornmeal.

Mix the dough until smooth and comes clean from the sides of the bowl.

If too sticky, adjust with a bit of flour. Remove to a table and knead for a few minutes. Shape into 4 oz dough balls. Let rise over night in the fridge.

Roll out to 10 to 12 inches very thin.

Sear quickly on grill top and cool.

UNDER THE SEA

Western Light Lobster Roll

LOBSTER SALAD WITH A TOUCH OF TARRAGON
ON A FRESH BAKED CROISSANT

We give our lobster roll a twist by serving it on a fresh baked super light croissant rather that the usual hot dog bun. Currently, it is not uncommon to see it presented on gluten free bread.

Serves 8

8 3½ oz croissants – fresh baked

3 lbs lobster meat – body and claws, cut in bite size chunks

1 cup mayonnaise

4 tbsp lemon juice – fresh squeezed

4 celery stalks – finely chopped (use centre stalks)

2 tbsp tarragon leaves – chopped

2 tbsp parsley leaves – chopped

   Salt and pepper

In a bowl, combine the lobster meat, mayonnaise, lemon juice, celery, tarragon, parsley, and salt and pepper to taste.

Cut the croissant horizontal to open and spoon in a generous amount of lobster filling.

Eel Lake Oysters on the Half Shell

PICKLED RIDGEVIEW APPLES,
PEPPERED STRAWBERRY VODKA GRANITE

We are lucky to be supplied directly to the door by Eel Lake Oysters, about an hour from Digby, with juicy fat oysters that don't disappoint. Guests of The Pines rave about the quality, whether served chilled on ice, or served as a hot appetizer.

For 36 Oysters

36 Oysters
Pickled Ridgeview Apples
Peppered Strawberry Vodka Granite

Wash and scrub the oysters until clean. Using a proper oyster shucking knife, pop open the oyster at the heel joint. Slide your knife across the underside of the top shell to release the oyster meat. Discard the top shell. Gently slide the oyster knife down into the bottom shell and release the meat there as well. Oysters are best served on crushed ice with assorted condiments.

PICKLED RIDGEVIEW APPLES

- 1 cup apple cider
- ½ cup cider vinegar
- ½ inch thick slice of fresh ginger
- ¼ tbsp allspice berries
- ¾ cup sugar
- 1 lbs apples – peeled, seeded and quartered
- 1 whole cinnamon stick

In a large nonreactive saucepan, combine the cider, vinegar, ginger, allspice, and sugar. Heat the mixture over low heat, stirring until the sugar is dissolved. Increase the heat and boil the syrup for 10 minutes.

Add the apples to the syrup and simmer them for 10 minutes. Transfer the apples to a cooling container and add the cinnamon stick. Boil the cider mixture for 10 minutes more and pour over the top of the apples. Let cool completely and then store.

PEPPERED STRAWBERRY VODKA GRANITE

- 4 tbsp sugar
- 4 cups ripe strawberries – washed and hulled
- 1 tbsp lemon juice – fresh squeezed
- 2 tbsp vodka
- ½ tsp cracked black pepper

To make the sugar syrup, combine ¾ cup water and 4 tbsp sugar in a small saucepan. Cook over medium heat, stirring until sugar has dissolved, about 2 minutes. Cool to room temperature.

Place half the strawberries in a blender with the sugar syrup, lemon juice and vodka. Purée. Transfer to a fine mesh sieve and press on purée, pushing the pulp through. Discard seeds remaining in sieve.

Pour mixture in a shallow 8 inch square pan. Add the cracked black peppercorns. Freeze 2 to 3 hours, or until almost completely frozen. Scrape granite with a fork to make it flaky. Freeze for another hour and scrape again. When ready to serve, scrape again.

Chilled Grilled Asparagus and Black Tiger Shrimp

DULSE MAYO, CERTIFIED ORGANIC MICRO GREENS, SWEET N' SOUR FISH SAUCE

This dish promotes our local certified organic greens. Always versatile organic greens, they can be used in several applications where small amounts of greens are features or used as a garnish.

Serves 8

40 asparagus spears – cut 4 inches in length, quickly boiled and cooled

24 pieces 21/25 black tiger shrimp

1 lb certified organic micro greens including snow pea shoots – 2 oz per plate

16 tbsp Dulse Mayo

8 tbsp Sweet n' Sour Fish Sauce

Season shrimp with salt, pepper and chopped garlic and sear quickly on a barbecue or grill. While the barbecue is hot, sear the asparagus spears as well and set aside.

Arrange some of the certified organic greens on each plate. Fan 5 pieces of the asparagus on each plate and sit the shrimp tail ends up. Streak some of the dulse mayo around the plate and spoon the sweet n' sour fish sauce around as well as some onto the greens.

DULSE MAYO

2 cups mayonnaise

½ cup dulse – dampen with water and chop fine

3 tbsp mirin (sweetened rice wine)

¼ cup rice vinegar

Combine all the ingredients in a bowl and stir well. Let rest to incorporate the flavours.

SWEET N' SOUR FISH SAUCE

makes 2 cups

1 cup sugar

½ cup rice wine vinegar

½ cup tomato juice

2 tsp fresh lemon juice

1 tbsp fish sauce – available in Asian food markets

Combine the sugar and the vinegar. Cook over medium-high heat until the mixture turns amber in color and then remove the saucepan from the heat.

Slowly and carefully whisk in the tomato juice, lemon juice and fish sauce.

The sauce can be made up to 5 days in advance.

Panko Crusted Crab Cakes

GRILLED ROMAINE, PICKLED EGGPLANT STIR FRY,
HONEY MUSTARD STREAKER

Crab Cakes are one of the staples of most restaurant menus in Atlantic Canada. It is no different here at the Digby Pines. Don't let the curry powder scare you. There is not enough there to dominate the flavor, but it will help accentuate all the other flavors in the cake. Crab cakes are on our menu almost every summer, but I change the sauces and accompaniments for our regular clients who visit us each year. It is also healthy for our chefs to prepare and execute a new variation each summer.

Makes 8 crab cakes

1 lb crab meat, squeeze to remove excess juice

2 eggs, slightly beaten

3 tbsp green onion, chopped

Juice from one lemon

1 tsp curry powder

4 tbsp mayonnaise

2 tbsp chopped parsley

1½ tsp Dijon mustard

½ cup bread crumbs

Salt and pepper

to cook

½ cup cornmeal

½ cup bread crumbs

to serve

2 heads romaine lettuce

Canola oil

2 cups mayonnaise

3 tbsp red wine vinegar

4 tbsp Dijon mustard

½ cup honey

Salt and pepper

Pickled Eggplant Stir Fry

CRAB CAKES: In a stainless-steel bowl, add all the ingredients and mix well to combine. Shape into 2 oz pucks and refrigerate to firm up.

Option 1 Mix cornmeal and bread crumbs well. Roll crab cakes in the mixture and pan fry to golden brown.

Option 2 Set up egg wash station of seasoned flour, egg wash and Panko bread crumbs.

Roll the crab cake in the flour, dredge through the egg wash and finish by rolling in the Panko bread crumbs.

Deep fry at 350°F until golden brown.

TO SERVE: Make the grilled romaine by brushing the romaine lightly with canola oil, season with salt and pepper, and grill quickly to get light grill marks.

Whisk together mayonnaise, red wine vinegar, Dijon, honey, salt and pepper in a stainless-steel bowl. Taste and adjust seasoning as needed.

PICKLED EGGPLANT STIR FRY

1 cup Pickled Eggplant , cut in thin strips

½ medium red onion, julienned

1 cup snow peas, julienned

1 cup red pepper (1 average size red pepper), julienned

1 cup yellow pepper (1 average size yellow pepper), julienned

Canola oil

Salt and pepper

In a very hot fry pan or wok, add the canola oil and heat until almost smoky. Add all the ingredients and flip fry several times. Season with salt and pepper to taste.

PICKLED EGGPLANT

4-5 medium-small eggplants (about 2 lbs in total)

2 tbsp salt

1 cup apple cider vinegar (white vinegar is fine)

2 cups water

3 tbsp fresh chopped parsley (or 1 tbsp dry)

2 tbsp fresh chopped basil (or 1 tbsp dry)

¼ cup chopped sweet or hot red pepper
(or 1 tsp hot pepper flakes)

3-4 cloves of garlic, minced

1-2 cups of extra virgin olive oil

Peel the eggplants, cut off the ends, and slice lengthwise into ½ inch slices. Cut these slices across, lengthwise again, to obtain long strips the size of skinny fries. Cut them in half if they're too long.

Place the slices in a colander with a bowl underneath the catch the liquid. Sprinkle with the salt and mix with your hands, giving your eggplant slices a little massage so they are evenly covered in salt. Allow them to sit for 3 to 4 hours, mixing and squeezing the liquid out with your hands every hour or so. You can also place a weight on top to help get the liquid out (a plate topped with a big bag of flour works well).

After 3 to 4 hours, rinse the slices well with tap water and drain. Squeeze as much liquid out of the eggplant slices as you can, using your hands. Place the squeezed eggplant aside.

Bring the vinegar and water to a boil. Place the eggplant slices in the boiling mixture and boil for about 2½ minutes. Do not leave in the boiling water longer than 3 minutes or the eggplant will be mushy. It should still have some bite to it. After about 2½ minutes, remove the eggplant from the liquid and drain. Once they are cool enough to handle, squeeze out any excess liquid with your hands again (you can also leave the slices to dry for a few minutes on a clean towel, wrapping them in the towel to press some of the liquid out). They don't have to be fully dry but they shouldn't be dripping wet.

Stuff the eggplant into clean jars, alternating in layers with the chopped parsley and basil, chopped red pepper, and minced garlic. Press down so that everything is well packed. Pour olive oil into the jar until all the ingredients are covered. Press down with a spoon to remove any air bubbles in the jar. Add extra olive if needed, leaving about ¾ inch of space at the top. Wipe the rims and close the jars. Keep in the fridge for up to 1 week, or freeze.

½ cup sliced onions

8 oz smoked haddock fillets

4 oz haddock fillets

2 cups of boiled, roughly mashed
  Yukon gold potatoes – drained well
  and cooled

½ cup finely chopped celery

1 egg – well beaten

  Panko bread crumbs

  Blanched asparagus tips

2 seedless oranges

  Peppered Tuna Aioli

  Pickled Rainbow Swiss Chard

Smoked Haddock Fish Cakes

ASPARAGUS TIPS, PEPPERED TUNA AIOLI,
ORANGE FILLETS, SWEET N' SOUR SWISS CHARD

We also use the local smoked haddock for this "out of the box" fish cake recipe. The subtle smoky flavour pairs well with the sweet and sour of the condiments, the richness of the aioli and the juicy citrus of the orange.

Serves 8

Lay the haddock out on a sheet pan and spread the onions around and over. Sprinkle lightly with salt and pepper. Bake 15 minutes at 350°F. Remove from oven and cool.

Fry the celery until soft. While the celery is frying, chop and add the onions that have been baked with the smoked haddock. Salt and pepper — taste the mixture and adjust seasoning.

Break up the haddock into a large stainless-steel bowl. Add in the celery and onions, potato and the egg. Season to taste. Mix to incorporate and scoop out into 16 (1 to 1½ oz) portions. Using your hands, shape into small cakes. Lightly press the cakes into the panko bread crumbs

Add a small amount of canola oil to a non-stick fry pan and fry the fish cakes to a nice golden colour. Keep warm in the oven. Meanwhile, warm the asparagus tips in butter and season with salt and pepper.

Trim the ends off each orange. With a paring knife, slice off the skin just underneath the pith but not too much into the orange flesh. Then, gently slice the wedges out between the white membrane that actually holds the sections together so that there is no white pith attached.

Spread a tbsp of the tuna aioli onto 8 plates and place two fish cakes onto the plate. Garnish with the asparagus tips, orange fillets and swiss chard.

PEPPERED TUNA AIOLI

- 3 oz good quality canned tuna
- 2 tbsp capers – rinsed
- 1 tbsp white wine vinegar
- 1 tbsp lemon juice
- 2 large egg yolks
- 1 cup canola oil
-   Salt and pepper

In a blender, combine the tuna, capers, vinegar, lemon juice and egg yolks.

Blend on high speed. Slowly drizzle in the olive and canola oils to form an emulsion. If the mixture becomes too thick, add a splash of water to achieve the correct consistency. Season with salt and pepper.

PICKLED RAINBOW SWISS CHARD

- 2 lbs rainbow Swiss chard stems – cut in small sections
- 2 cups white wine vinegar
- 2 cups apple cider vinegar
- 2 cups sugar
- 1 tbsp mustard seeds
- 4 bay leaves
- 1 tbsp black peppercorns
- 1 piece star anise
- 8 whole cloves

Put the sliced rainbow chard into containers.

Bring all ingredients to a boil to dissolve the sugar and blend the flavors and pour over the Swiss chard. Refrigerate to cool and then cover.

Non-Traditional Shrimp Cocktail

LIME GINGER MARINATED WATERMELON, FETA CHEESE,
SHAVED ARUGULA, GRILLED PINEAPPLE COCKTAIL SAUCE

This 'shrimp cocktail with a twist' appeared on our 2017 menu
and will appear again in 2018. It is a spin on an old classic,
but perfect for the summer.

Serves 8

40 large Poached Tiger Shrimp

4 cups baby arugula

8 heaping tbsp Grilled Pineapple Cocktail Sauce

8 oz feta cheese – crumbled

½ large seedless watermelon –
peeled and cut in 1½ inch cubes

4 tbsp grated fresh ginger

4 limes – cut in half

Put the watermelon in a large bowl and add the grated ginger and lime juice. Gently stir the watermelon to gather up some of the ginger and lime.

On 8 plates, spoon and streak some of the cocktail sauce. Place seven pieces of the marinated watermelon in a pile in the center of the plate. Arrange five tiger shrimp randomly around and on the watermelon. Sprinkle the feta cheese over and around the shrimp and watermelon. Pile a small handful of the arugula on top of the watermelon.

GRILLED PINEAPPLE COCKTAIL SAUCE

1 small fresh pineapple –
cored and cut in slices

1 cup chili sauce

1 cup ketchup

6 tbsp prepared horseradish

4 tsp lemon juice

1 tsp Worcestershire sauce

½ tsp tabasco sauce

For the cocktail sauce, combine the chili sauce, ketchup, horseradish, lemon juice, Worcestershire sauce, and hot sauce. Grill the slices of pineapple and chop into very small pieces and mix into the sauce.

POACHED TIGER SHRIMP

- 1 **lemon – juice only**
- 1 **medium onion – coarse chopped**
- 1 **small carrot – peeled and coarse chopped**
- 6 **bay leaves**
- 1 **tbsp black peppercorns**
  Kosher salt
  Tiger shrimp – 40 pieces peeled and deveined

Bring a large pot of water to a vigorous boil. Add the lemon juice, onion, carrots, bay leaves, peppercorns and salt. Simmer for 20 minutes to build the flavors. Add the shrimp and cook, uncovered, for only 3 minutes, until the shrimp are just cooked through. Remove with a slotted spoon to a bowl of cold water. Remove and keep cold until ready to serve.

Cedar Plank Smoked Salmon and Shrimp

ARUGULA, SPINACH, FRIED PROSCUITTO, PINE NUTS, DRIED FIGS

Serves 8

1 lb Smoked Salmon – broken into large pieces

24 pcs 21/25 tiger shrimp – smoked (season with salt and pepper and put in smoker along with salmon)

4 cups mixture of baby arugula greens and spinach

8 slices of proscuitto – cut in small pieces and dried in the oven 250°F (40 min)

½ cup pine nuts – toasted

8 dried figs – cut in quarters

Dulse Ranch Dressing

Arrange some of the arugula and spinach onto the center of each plate.

Divide the smoked salmon over the top of the greens. Place the shrimp around the plate. Sprinkle with toasted pine nuts. Insert the pieces of dried proscuitto throughout the salad and garnish around the plate with pieces of the dried figs.

Serve with some of the dulse ranch dressing.

SMOKED SALMON

1 cedar plank 6 × 1 × 24 inches – pre-bake the plank over a gas burner or in the oven to activate cedar oils.

1 salmon fillet – about 2 lbs

DRY CURE

8 oz salt

4 oz sugar

2 tsp onion powder

¾ tsp ground cloves

¾ tsp ground or crushed bay leaf

¾ tsp ground mace

¾ tsp ground all spice

Remove the pin bones from the salmon and center it skin side down on a large piece of cheesecloth. Mix the cure ingredients thoroughly and pack evenly over the salmon. The layer should be slightly thinner where the fillet tapers to the tail.

Wrap the salmon loosely in the cheesecloth and place it in a hotel pan. Cure the salmon under refrigeration for 12 to 24 hours. Gently rinse off the cure with cool water and blot dry. Air-dry, uncovered, on a rack under refrigeration overnight to form a pellicle (a tacky dry surface on the salmon). Place the salmon fillet on the cedar plank and hot smoke at 140°F for 45 minutes to 1 hour.

The smoked salmon is now ready for service, or it may be cooled, wrapped and stored for up to 1 week.

DULSE RANCH DRESSING

½ cup mayonnaise

¾ cup sour cream

¾ cup buttermilk

1 tbsp white wine vinegar

1 tbsp lemon juice

1½ tbsp Worcestershire sauce

2 tsp chopped parsley

2 tsp chopped chives

1 clove garlic – crushed

½ scallion – chopped

¼ cup dulse – chopped (dampen the dulse a little with water, it is easier to chop)

Put all the ingredients into a bowl and stir well to incorporate.

Steamed Ship Harbour Mussels on the Half Shell

SHIITAKE MUSHROOM COLESLAW, CROUTON BITS, DILL BUTTER SAUCE

Mussels are a very versatile seafood and can be used in everything from iconic chowders to stuffing for game birds. They are cheap and plentiful around the shores of Nova Scotia and Atlantic Canada, but we buy farmed mussels.

Serves 4

1 oz canola oil
1 tbsp shallots – chopped small
2 tsp garlic – chopped
4 lbs fresh mussels
4 oz white wine
Salt and pepper
Shiitake Mushroom Coleslaw
Dill Butter Sauce

On medium high heat, in a large sauce pot, heat the canola oil and add in the shallots. Fry the shallots briefly and add in the garlic and mussels. Stir the mussels in with the onions and garlic, add in the white wine and cover immediately with a tight lid. Steam for two minutes or until all the mussels have popped open.

Serve the mussels on the half shell around a plate. Garnish the center of the plate with some of the shiitake mushroom coleslaw and drizzle the dill butter sauce over and around the mussels.

Sprinkle with a few croutons.

SHIITAKE MUSHROOM COLESLAW

¼ cup red wine vinegar
¼ cup cider vinegar
1 tbsp honey
1 lb shiitake mushroom caps – stems removed; cut in thin julienne and sautéed
½ head green cabbage – thinly sliced
½ head red cabbage – thinly sliced
½ red onion – thinly sliced
1 carrot – peeled and grated
Kosher salt and black pepper
½ cup mayonnaise
Pinch of cayenne pepper

Combine the vinegars in a small saucepan and reduce by half over medium heat.

Remove from the heat and stir in the honey. Allow to cool to room temperature.

In a large bowl, combine the shiitake mushrooms, red and green cabbage, onion, and carrot. Pour in the vinegar mixture, season with salt and pepper, and mix well. Allow the mixture to sit for 10 minutes, mixing again after 5 minutes.

Stir in the mayonnaise and cayenne. Adjust the seasoning if necessary.

DILL BUTTER SAUCE

⅔ cup white wine
1½ tsp shallots – chopped
1 tbsp lemon juice – freshly squeezed
1 tbsp fresh dill – chopped
⅔ cup 35% cream
1 cup unsalted butter
Salt and pepper to taste

In a saucepan over medium heat, add wine, shallots and lemon juice and reduce volume by half. Add the dill and cream and reduce for another five minutes. Cut the butter into cubes and add slowly to the cream mixture over medium heat, whisking until a smooth sauce is obtained. Season to taste.

Signature Smoked Haddock and Bacon Chowder

FRESH THYME, ONIONS, POTATOES, CREAMY SEAFOOD BROTH

Chowders are unique to every household and community in Atlantic Canada. No two are the same, nor should they be. Our smoked haddock is prepared by Fundy Fisheries about 10 km from the Pines as the crow flies, but about 45 minutes to drive.

Serves 8

¼ **lb butter**

2 **cups white onion – diced**

1 **cup diced celery**

1 **lb raw bacon – cooked almost crispy and cut in half inch pieces**

1 **lb smoked haddock**

1 **tbsp dried thyme**

¾ **cup rice flour**

4 **cups fish stock (or water if necessary)**

4 **medium sized Yukon gold potatoes – cut in small chunks,**

Finish Chowder with:

 35% cream

 Salt and pepper to taste

Melt butter in pan. Sauté onions, celery, bacon and thyme in butter until all is translucent, about 5 minutes. Add the smoke haddock.

Dust with rice flour.

Add the fish stock a little at a time, stirring to incorporate and avoid lumping.

In a separate pot or steamer, cook potatoes until tender and add to finished chowder. Finish with cream and season with salt and pepper to taste.

TIP: Thickening with rice flour keeps the chowder gluten free

Breaded Haddock Tacos

NAPA CABBAGE SLAW, PICKLED GINGER,
LEMON GARLIC AIOLI

Serves 8

16 2 oz strips of haddock about 4 inches long and ¼ inch thick

2 tbsp paprika

1 tsp salt

½ tsp pepper

1 cup all-purpose flour

2 eggs – well beaten with a little bit of water to be used for egg wash

2 cups panko bread crumbs

1 quart of canola oil

16 6 inch flour tortillas

2 oz pickled ginger – cut in very thin strips

Lemon Garlic Aioli (see Recipe Appendix page 120)

Pickled Napa Cabbage Slaw – prepare ahead of time

Mix the paprika, salt and pepper with the flour.

Set up a breading station of consecutive containers for the flour mixture, beaten egg, and the panko bread crumbs.

Drag the haddock strips through the flour a few pieces at a time, dredge into the egg wash and toss in the panko to coat evenly. Place them on a tray until you have breaded all the haddock strips.

Heat the canola oil in a sauce pot, or countertop deep fryer, to 350°F. Fry the haddock strips a few at a time to a golden brown. They will cook by the time they are golden brown.

Grill the flour tortillas briefly. Spoon some lemon garlic aioli on each tortilla, followed by one strip of haddock. Cover with some Napa Cabbage Slaw. Sprinkle with some pickled ginger. Fold and serve.

PICKLED NAPA CABBAGE SLAW

½ cup rice vinegar

¼ cup plus 2 tbsp sugar

1 tbsp ginger – finely chopped

2 tsp salt

½ tsp garlic – finely chopped

3 whole cloves

5 medium carrots – cut in 3 × ⅛ inch julienne

¾ lb snow peas – cut in julienne

1¼ lb napa cabbage – leaves halved lengthwise, then cut crosswise into ¼ inch strips

2 tbsp jalapeno pepper – seeded and thinly sliced julienne

Bring vinegar, sugar, ginger, salt, garlic, and cloves to a boil in a small saucepan, stirring until sugar is dissolved, then remove from heat and let steep, uncovered, 30 minutes. Discard cloves.

While pickling liquid steeps, blanch carrots in a 6- to 8-quart pot of boiling salted water 30 seconds, then transfer with a large slotted spoon to a bowl of ice and cold water to stop cooking. Lift out carrots with slotted spoon and drain in a colander. Transfer to paper towels and pat dry.

Blanch snow peas in same pot of boiling water 30 seconds, then transfer to ice water, drain, and pat dry in same manner. Cut each snow pea lengthwise into 4 strips.

Blanch cabbage in same pot of boiling water 5 seconds, then transfer to ice water, drain, and pat dry.

Just before serving, toss vegetables with pickling liquid and jalapeno in a large bowl.

LEMON GARLIC AIOLI

see Recipe Appendix page 120

Maple and Cashew Crusted Atlantic Salmon

DRIED FRUIT AND BERRY QUINOA, SWEET N' SOUR RADISH, BUTTERED BABY CARROTS

Feel free to use any carrot you like with this dish. Science has developed beautiful artisan carrots, yellow, purple and red. Of course, there are orange ones of every shape and size.

Serves 8

8 5 oz portions of Atlantic salmon
   Salt and pepper
1 oz canola oil
2 oz maple syrup
½ cup unsalted cashews – chopped fine
½ cup panko bread crumbs
¼ cup melted butter
   Dried Fruit and Berry Quinoa
   Sweet n' Sour Radish
   Lemon Butter Sauce (see Recipe Appendix page 120)

Mix the chopped cashews with the butter and bread crumbs

Preheat the oven to 350°F.

Season the salmon with salt and pepper. Heat the canola oil in a frying pan and sear the salmon to a golden brown. Set aside to cool.

When the salmon is cool, brush it with maple syrup and press some of the bread crumb/panko mixture onto the top of the salmon. The maple syrup will help it adhere to the surface of the salmon.

Bake the salmon in the oven until the white fat starts to break through the layers on the sides. The salmon will be medium rare internally. If you prefer it more well done, leave it in the oven longer.

Scoop some of the quinoa onto the center of each plate. Place the salmon on top of the quinoa. Warm some radishes and carrots in butter, salt and pepper and distribute around the salmon plate. Spoon a bit of the lemon butter sauce over and around the salmon.

DRIED FRUIT AND BERRY QUINOA

1 oz canola oil
½ medium onion – diced small
2 cups dried quinoa – white or red
1 cup vegetable stock
1 cup orange juice
¼ cup butter
½ cup dried apricots – cut in ¼ inch dice
½ cup dried cranberries – chopped in small pieces
¼ cup dried wild blueberries
¼ cup raisins
   Salt and pepper

In a medium size sauce pot, heat the canola oil and add the onion. Stir the onion and cook until translucent about 5 to 6 minutes. Add the quinoa and stir for 30 seconds. Add the vegetable stock and the orange juice. Bring to a boil and cover with the lid of the pot about 20 minutes. When the quinoa has absorbed all the stock, remove from the heat and stir in the butter and the dried fruits and berries.

Season with salt and pepper and set aside.

SWEET N' SOUR RADISH

2 cups red radish – ends sliced off. If the radishes are large, cut them in half.

½ medium onion – sliced

3 cups water

1 cup brown sugar

1 cup red wine vinegar

Juice from half lemon

Bring the water, brown sugar, red wine vinegar and lemon juice to a boil. Add in the onions and radishes. Turn to a simmer and cook the radishes until slightly softened. Cool completely in the stock. Reserve the stock for future use.

LEMON BUTTER SAUCE
See Recipe Appendix page 120

Butter Poached Fundy Lobster on Roasted Tomato Risotto

BASIL CREAM SAUCE, OVEN DRIED TOMATO, FENNEL, TRUFFLE OLIVE OIL, SHAVED PADANO PARMESAN

Truffle oil can be expensive and the flavour is very robust, so you can stretch your truffle oil by cutting it 60/40 with extra virgin olive oil. Spoon over top of the finished risotto.

Serves 8

4 2 lb lobster – ½ lb each serving
1 bulb fennel – finely cut across the bulb to create half-moon irregular shapes
   Risotto
   Oven Dried Tomatoes
   Basil Cream Sauce (see Recipe Appendix page 120)

Cook lobsters and remove all the meat. Chop the tail meat into small pieces and reserve the claw meat to garnish the top of the risotto. Add the tail meat to the risotto just before adding the cheese and butter. Warm the claw pieces in melted butter and garnish over the risotto.

Blanch fennel in boiling salted water for 45 seconds. Scoop out into ice water to stop the cooking. Before serving, warm the fennel in a little butter and season with salt and pepper.

Divide the risotto into serving bowls. Place a nice amount of fennel on top and garnish with the warm dried tomato wedges and the buttered lobster claw meat. Spoon some of the basil cream sauce around the risotto and serve.

RISOTTO

5 shallots – finely chopped
5 cloves garlic – finely chopped
¼ cup white wine
1 lb Arborio rice
8 cups vegetable stock – pre-boiled
   Salt and pepper
½ cup Padano parmesan cheese – grated
6 tbsp unsalted butter

TIP: Never boil the rice. Let the stock absorb slowly as not to damage the integrity of the rice kernel.

In a large sauce pan, lightly sauté the shallots and garlic until cooked through, add white wine and reduce until there is not much left in the pot.

Add risotto rice to the cooked shallots. Season the rice with salt and pepper and stir for one minute. Add the vegetable stock slowly and stir until all is absorbed. Continue to add the vegetable stock and stir until the rice is a firm al dente.

Finish with some parmesan cheese and unsalted butter and adjust seasoning.

OVEN DRIED TOMATOES

(an overnight process)

4 medium sized tomatoes – core removed and cut in 8 wedges
2 tbsp canola oil
1 tbsp dried basil

Preheat oven to 150°F.

Toss the tomato wedges in the canola oil and dried basil. Place on a baking sheet and place in the oven overnight. Remove from oven and cool until ready to use. Warm dried tomato in the oven, or use a microwave to reheat and garnish top of the risotto.

BASIL CREAM SAUCE
See Recipe Appendix page 120

Pan Fried Haddock with Citrus Salsa

POTATO AND CAULIFLOWER PURÉE, BUTTERED FENNEL,
SWISS CHARD, PINOT GRIS BUTTER

Serves 8

Canola oil for frying

8   6–8oz fillets haddock, cut in half

Rice flour seasoned with salt and pepper – for dredging

2   cups Potato and Cauliflower Purée

1   bulb fennel – shaved across the bulb to create little pieces

8   cups Swiss chard – washed and chopped, leaves and stems together

8   oz Pinot Gris Butter

Citrus Salsa

Dredge the haddock through the rice flour. Add some oil to a large fry pan and turn the heat on medium high. Pan fry the haddock to a light brown and turn the fillets over and cook from the other side. About ½ minute each side.

Spoon some of the warm potato cauliflower purée onto the plates. Saute the shaved fennel in butter to soften and pile on the plate beside the purée. Twist some of the Swiss chard into a little pile beside the fennel.

Stack two of the haddock portions off set between the fennel and Swiss chard. Top with the citrus salsa and some of the butter sauce.

POTATO CAULIFLOWER PURÉE

1½   lbs fresh cauliflower – cut in small pieces

½   lb white potatoes – peeled and cut in small pieces

¼   to ½ cup milk

2   tbsp butter

Salt and pepper to taste

Boil the vegetables until tender, about 15 minutes for the cauliflower and 30 minutes for the potatoes.

Drain the vegetables and purée them together in a food processor. The purée should be moist enough, but if it isn't, add some milk.

Stir in the butter and season with the salt and pepper. Blend well. (The purée can be made a day or two in advance and refrigerated. Reheat in a water bath or microwave oven.

PINOT GRIS BUTTER SAUCE

⅔   cup Pinot Gris white wine

1½   tsp shallots – chopped

1   tbsp lemon juice – freshly squeezed

⅔   cup 35% cream

1   cup unsalted butter

Salt and pepper to taste

In a saucepan over medium heat, add wine, shallots and lemon juice and reduce volume by half. Add the cream and reduce for another five minutes. Cut the butter into cubes and add slowly to the cream mixture over medium heat, whisking until a smooth sauce is obtained. Season to taste.

CITRUS SALSA

½   cup thinly sliced red onion

1   cup grapefruit sections

1   cup orange sections

½   cup lemon sections

¼   cup flat leaf parsley – chopped

¼   cup cilantro – chopped

½   tbsp fresh lime juice

2   tbsp olive oil

Salt and pepper

Combine the ingredients and fold together. Season with salt and pepper.

Pan Seared Digby Scallops and Scrunchions

YUKON GOLD HASH BROWNS, CARROT TARRAGON MASH, BUTTERED GREEN BEANS

'Scrunchions' are a food group in Newfoundland. They are essentially little flavor bags of rendered salt pork backfat. They make a nice flavor hit along with the rich scallops.

Serves 8

- 3 tbsp canola oil
- 3 lbs 'World Famous' Digby Scallops – 10/20 grade
- 1 medium onion – diced small
- 4 large Yukon gold potatoes – washed and cut in half inch cubes
  Carrot Tarragon Mash
- 2 tbsp butter
- 1 lb fresh green beans – pre-cooked
  Lemon Butter Sauce
  Scrunchions

In a large fry pan, add the canola oil, season the scallops, and sear to a golden brown. About 1 minute on each side. Set aside to keep warm but don't overcook them.

For the hash browns, heat some canola oil in a large non-stick fry pan. On a medium-high heat, fry the onion along with the potatoes to put some good color on the potatoes. Turn the heat down and continue to fry until the potatoes and onions are cooked and nicely browned.

Warm the carrot tarragon mash and heat the green beans in a bit of butter. Season with salt and pepper.

On each plate, spoon a nice amount of potato hash browns. Place a few green beans criss-cross over the potatoes. Scoop two little piles of the carrot tarragon mash on each plate. Arrange the scallops randomly around the plate and sprinkle with some of the pork scrunchions. Drizzle with a little butter sauce and enjoy!

LEMON BUTTER SAUCE

- ⅔ cup white wine
- 1½ tsp shallots, chopped
- 1 tbsp lemon juice – freshly squeezed
- ⅔ cup 35% cream
- 1 cup unsalted butter
  Salt and pepper to taste

In a saucepan over medium heat, add wine, shallots and lemon juice and reduce volume by half. Add the cream and reduce for another five minutes. Cut the butter into cubes and add slowly to the cream mixture over medium heat, whisking until a smooth sauce is obtained. Season to taste.

SCRUNCHIONS

- ½ lb salt pork back fat – skin removed

Cut pork fatback into small cubes. Add to skillet; fry at low to medium heat until fat is rendered out and fatback is crispy and golden brown. You can drain the initial liquid periodically given off by the pork fat. (Don't overheat or the fat will burn.) Remove pork scrunchions; set aside.

CARROT TARRAGON MASH

- 4 medium carrots – peeled and cut in small pieces
- 1 tbsp fresh tarragon – chopped
- 2 tsp honey
- 2 tbsp butter
  Salt and pepper

Boil the carrots until soft. Drain the water and mash the carrots with fresh tarragon, honey and butter. Season with salt and pepper.

Pan Seared "World Famous" Digby Scallops

Risotto, risotto, risotto. Every season we feature a risotto of some kind on our Churchill's menu. On these four pages we showcase two of our seasonal scallop dishes. Start with the scallops and risotto, then add the flavours of your choice.

Risotto is sacred to Italians who are passionate about the preparation, execution and delivery of this product. Respect the kernel!

Serves 8

SCALLOPS

Using large Digby Scallops, season lightly with salt and pepper and fry in a frying pan over high heat. Sear one side until golden and turn briefly to sear the other side. Serve around the risotto immediately.

WILD MUSHROOM RISOTTO

- 5 shallots – finely chopped
- 5 cloves garlic – finely chopped
- 8 oz mixed wild mushrooms cut or ripped into small pieces (shiitake, oyster, portobello, button mushrooms)
- 3 oz white wine
- 1 lb Arborio rice
- 8 cups vegetable stock – pre-boiled
- Salt and pepper
- ½ cup Padano parmesan cheese – grated
- 6 tbsp unsalted butter

In a large sauce pan, lightly sautée the shallots and garlic until cooked through, then add mushrooms and cook until soft, add white wine and reduce until there is not much left in the pot.

Add risotto rice to the cooked shallot and mushroom. Season the rice with salt and pepper and stir for one minute. Add the vegetable stock slowly and stir until all is absorbed. Continue to add the vegetable stock and stir until the rice is a firm al dente.

TIP: Never boil the rice. Let the stock absorb slowly as not to damage the integrity of the rice kernel.

Finish with some parmesan cheese and unsalted butter and adjust seasoning.

2016 Digby Scallops

WILD MUSHROOM RISOTTO, GRILLED CORN PURÉE, GREEN PEA SAUCE, LEMON MASCARPONE

GRILLED CORN PURÉE

- 3 cobs of corn – husked, boiled and cooled
- 1 medium onion – cut in rings
- 2 tbsp canola oil
  Salt and pepper
- 2 cups vegetable stock

Brush the corn cobs with canola oil and toss the onion in the same oil. Season with salt and pepper. Roll the corn around on a very hot grill until the corn has good markings on it. Grill the onion. Cut the corn off the cob and add the corn and onions to a medium sauce pot. Add the vegetable stock and bring to a boil and cook until the corn is soft. Purée until very smooth. Adjust seasoning.

GREEN PEA PURÉE

- 2 tbsp canola oil
- 1 medium onion – diced small
- 4 cups frozen peas
- 2 cups vegetable stock
  Salt and pepper

In a medium sauce pan, heat the oil and add the onions. Sweat the onions 5 to 7 minutes until translucent. Add the peas and vegetable stock and bring it to a boil.

Season with salt and pepper. Bring to a boil and cook for 3 to 4 minutes. Purée until very smooth and adjust seasoning.

LEMON MASCARPONE CHEESE

- 2 cups 35% cream
- 1 tbsp lemon juice

In a large saucepan, heat the cream over medium heat until it reaches 190°F. Stir in the lemon juice and continue to simmer for 5 minutes, taking care to maintain 190°F. The mixture will thicken to the consistency of gravy. Remove from the heat and allow to cool completely.

Line a fine mesh sieve with several layers of cheese cloth and place over a bucket or large bowl. Pour the cream mixture into the sieve and allow to drain in the fridge for 36 hours.

TIP: Cheese keeps, refrigerated, for up to 1 week. The liquid you catch in the bucket — whey — can be used to make polenta.

2017 Digby Scallops

WILD MUSHROOM RISOTTO, FENNEL SAUSAGE, ROASTED GARLIC, TOMATO RAGOUT SAUCE

see photo page 61

PINES FENNEL SAUSAGE

- 4 lbs pork shoulder butts – cut in long strips that will fit the meat grinder.
- 1 oz Kosher salt – sprinkle the salt on the pork and refrigerate ½ hour
- 1 tbsp black pepper
- 2 tbsp Italian herbs (dried)
- 2 tbsp fennel seeds – toasted
- 1 tbsp anise seeds – toasted (grind half of the fennel seeds and anise seeds)
- ¼ cup garlic – chopped
- 1½ tbsp smoked paprika
- ¼ cup sugar
- ½ tsp cayenne pepper
  Salt – to taste

Set up the meat grinder using the medium coarse plate. Mix the black pepper, Italian herbs, fennel and anise seeds, chopped garlic, smoked paprika, sugar and cayenne pepper.

Do the first grind of the pork through the meat grinder. Sprinkle with the spice mixture and grind one more time.

Manually, mix the forcemeat with your hands until well combined.

Make a small patty taster and fry. Adjust seasoning if necessary.

TOMATO FENNEL RAGOUT

- 1 large onion – medium diced
- 2 tbsp garlic – chopped
- 1 cup fennel – cut in long strips
- 1 cup carrot – medium dice
- 1 tbsp basil
- 1½ tsp fennel or anise seed
- 1 100 oz can plum tomatoes
  Salt and pepper
- ¼ cup sugar
- 1 lb fennel sausage (out of the casings) – fried coarse and left separate.

In a large sauce pan, fry the onions and garlic 5 to 7 minutes. Turn down the temperature and add in the fennel, carrot, basil and fennel seed. Stir the mixture for 3 to 4 minutes to allow flavors to develop.

Strain the tomatoes and reserve the juice. Chop the plum tomatoes into small pieces and add to the pan. Bring to a boil and reduce heat to simmer. Season the mixture with salt and pepper and simmer for 15 minutes. Add the sugar, simmer 5 more minutes and remove from heat.

FOR SERVICE: Add some of the ground fennel sausage to a serving of tomato ragout. Keeping the sausage separate gives you the ability to have this as a vegetarian dish.

Seared Peppered Halibut

CANDIED PECAN LEEK POTATO CAKE, CARDAMOM
GLAZED CARROTS, RHUBARB JAM, LEMON BUTTER,
TARRAGON OIL

Imagine a 200 lb halibut arriving at the back door, caught fresh 8 hours earlier. These are the exciting moments chefs live for, and a great learning opportunity for our co-op students.

Serves 8

8 6 oz portions of fresh Atlantic halibut preferably about 1 inch thick

1 oz canola oil

½ cup pink peppercorns

½ cup black peppercorns

Set your oven to 350°F.

Mix the peppercorns and grind. Press some of the peppercorn mix into the surface of the halibut. Season with salt, and sear in a fry pan to seal the surface. Turn the halibut over and sear the other side. Finish the halibut to medium (internal temperature of 130°F) in the oven.

Place the pecan and leek cake in the center of the plate. Pile a small amount of the carrots beside the potato cake and place the halibut on the potato cake, just touching the carrots. Spoon some of the rhubarb jam onto the front of the halibut, falling off onto the plate. Streak some butter sauce and tarragon oil around the plate.

CARDAMOM GLAZED CARROTS

1 oz canola oil

4 medium carrots – shredded into fine julienne on a mandolin

½ cup honey

1 tsp ground cardamom

In a medium fry pan, add the oil and fry the carrots. Add the honey and ground cardamom. Cook, stirring often, until the carrots start to wilt slightly. Serve immediately.

TARRAGON OIL

1 cup parsley – chopped

½ cup tarragon – chopped

1 cup canola oil

Salt and pepper

In a small blender purée all of the ingredients, along with a pinch of salt and pepper. Pass through a fine strainer and refrigerate.

CANDIED PECAN AND LEEK POTATO CAKE

2 lbs Yukon gold potatoes – prebaked and flesh removed

1 cup candied pecans – chopped into small pieces

1 oz canola oil

1 cup chopped leeks – use the white and light green parts.

Salt and pepper

Add the canola oil to a medium fry pan and saute the leeks until they are soft. Season along the way with salt and pepper.

Grate the potato flesh into a stainless steel bowl. Add in the leeks and pecans. Season with salt and pepper mix well.

Divide the mix into 8 equal portions. Squeeze the mix, and shape into hockey puck shapes.

Pan fry to a golden brown and hold for plating.

CANDIED PECANS

1 egg whites

2 cups pecans

1 tsp cinnamon

2 tbsp icing sugar

Preheat oven to 250°F.

Whisk the egg whites to a broken bubbly froth. Add the pecans, cinnamon and icing sugar and toss together.

Bake in the oven for 45 minutes, turning after 25 minutes. Cool and serve.

TIP: Pecans will be soft immediately from the oven, but will crisp as they cool.

LEMON BUTTER SAUCE
See Recipe Appendix page 120

SWEET N' SOUR RHUBARB CHUTNEY
See Recipe Appendix page 122

Haddock Salmon Fish Cake and Jumbo Tiger Shrimp

SPINACH GNOCCHI, BUTTERED ASPARAGUS,
SHAVED FENNEL, GRAPEFRUIT AND ALMOND BUTTER

Serves 8

1 bulb fennel

1 lb haddock and salmon – seasoned, baked and cooled

4 oz white bread cubes – crusts removed

3 oz grain mustard aioli

½ tbsp dried dill

Salt and pepper

Flour for dredging

24 large shrimp

Spinach Gnocchi

Grapefruit and Almond Butter

Finely cut fennel bulb across the bulb to create half-moon irregular shapes. Blanch in boiling salted water for 45 seconds. Scoop out into ice water to stop the cooking.

Combine the haddock, salmon and bread cubes. Add the aioli and dill to moisten and combine the fish and bread cubes. Add enough aioli so that the mixture stays together but is not too wet. You may not need all of the aioli. Season with the salt and pepper. Form into 3 oz pucks.

Dredge the fish cakes through flour and pan fry to golden brown. Place in center of the plate. Warm the shaved fennel in a little butter and season with salt and pepper.

Season shrimp with salt and pepper and grill quickly on both sides. Place the shrimp on and around the fish cake.

Pan fry the gnocchi in a non-stick fry pan in a small amount of canola oil until they begin to brown around the edges. Scatter around the plate. Spoon some of the grapefruit almond butter over and around the plate.

GRAPEFRUIT AND ALMOND BUTTER

1 tbsp butter

¼ cup onions – small diced

½ cup white wine

1 cup Ruby Red grapefruit juice

2-3 drops almond extract

1 tsp cornstarch

½ lb butter – cut in cubes

Salt and pepper

In a small sauce pan on medium high heat, melt 1 tbsp of butter along with the onions. Sweat the onions for 4 to 5 minutes. Add the white wine and reduce by half. Add the red grapefruit juice and almond extract and reduce the volume to about ¼ cup. Mix the cornstarch with a little bit of water and stir it into the red grapefruit reduction.

Reduce the heat to low and whisk in the ½ lb of butter cubes. Season to taste with salt and pepper. Spoon over and around fish cakes and shrimp.

SPINACH GNOCCHI

- 1 **cup all purpose flour**
- ¾ **cup plus 2 tbsp whole milk**
- 6 **tbsp unsalted butter – cut into pieces**
- 2 **oz Padano parmesan – finely grated**
- 2 **cups baby spinach – blanched, drained, squeezed and chopped fine**
- ¾ **tsp salt**
- ⅛ **tsp nutmeg**
- 3 **large eggs**

Sift the flour into a bowl. Bring the milk and butter just to a boil in a large sauce pan, stirring until butter is melted. Reduce heat, then, when mixture is at a simmer, add the flour all at once and cook, stirring vigorously with a wooden spoon, until the mixture pulls away from the side of the pan, 1 to 2 minutes. Remove from heat and stir in Padano parmesan, spinach, salt and nutmeg.

Add eggs one at a time, stirring vigorously after each addition until the mixture is smooth. Transfer dough to pastry bag.

Working in batches of about 20, pipe ½-inch lengths of dough directly into a 6 to 8 quart pot of poaching water, using scissors or paring knife to cut dough off at the tip.

Simmer gnocchi until they rise to surface, then transfer with a slotted spoon to a large bowl of ice water to stop cooking. Drain and lay out on an oiled baking sheet.

Fusilli Noodles with Smoked Atlantic Salmon

TOMATO VODKA CREAM, SNOW PEAS, TOMATO FILLETS

One of life's guilty pleasures is a big bowl of creamy pasta. The joy of eating it easily overcomes the guilt that goes along with it. I suggest a big fat piece of crusty garlic bread to help soak up the last of the garlicy tomato cream.

Serves 8

8	cups fusilli noodles – cooked
24	oz Tomato Vodka Cream Sauce
1	medium onion – cut in julienne
2	oz canola oil
16	oz Smoked AtlanticSalmon (see recipe page 45)
2	cups snow peas – pick the stem and stringy edge off each one. Cut in half lengthwise.
4	tomatoes – cut each tomato in six wedges. Cut the core off of the tomato wedges leaving a leaf-shaped wall of tomato flesh. Cut each leaf into three equal strips.
	Salt and pepper

In a large Dutch oven, add the canola oil and cook the onions until translucent, 4 to 5 minutes. Add in the smoked salmon and stir well. Season with a little salt and pepper. Add the snow peas and the vodka cream sauce and bring it to a boil. The cream is already reduced so will not need to boil very long. Add in the fusilli noodles and half of the tomato fillets. Stir together and adjust the seasoning.

Divide into eight pasta bowls and garnish with the remaining tomato fillets.

TOMATO VODKA CREAM SAUCE

1	oz canola oil
1	medium onion – peeled and diced
2	tsp garlic – chopped
½	cup white wine
3	tbsp tomato paste
¼	cup vodka
2	tbsp bottled pesto
4	cups 35% cream

In a medium sauce pan on medium high heat, saute the onions in the canola oil for five minutes. Add the garlic and sautée one more minute.

Add the white wine and reduce until it is almost all gone. Whisk in the tomato paste and add the vodka. Add in the pesto and the 35% cream. Whisk to incorporate and bring to a boil. Reduce the heat to medium low and reduce to about ¾ of the original volume. Check occasionally so that the cream doesn't boil and go over onto the stove. Remove from the heat and have ready to use in the pasta.

FOUR FEET ON THE GROUND

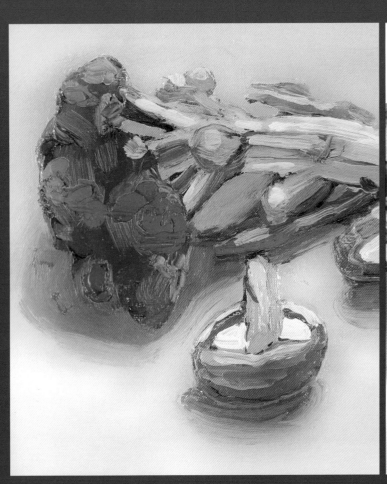

House-Made Charcuterie

COUNTRY PATE, DRIED SAUSAGE, DUCK PROSCUITTO, CURED HAM,
RED ONION BALSAMIC JAM, HOUSE PICKLES, MUSTARD TAPENADE, CROSTINI

House-made charcuterie is the number one menu item currently in restaurants. We are proud to say we make all of our own charcuterie meats and condiments. Enjoy with some fabulous Nova Scotia cheeses and red wine.

COUNTRY PATE

- ¾ cup brandy – boil and reduce to half cup
- 3 tbsp unsalted butter
- 1 cup onion – minced
- 2½ lbs ground pork
- 8-10 slices bacon – finely chopped, plus 14 bacon slices for lining the loaf pan
- 3 cloves garlic – finely chopped
- 2½ tsp salt
- 2½ tsp dried thyme
- 1 tsp anise seed
- 1½ tsp all spice
- 1 tsp ground black pepper
- 2 large eggs – beaten
- ⅓ cup 35% cream

In a small fry pan, melt the butter and add the onions. Cook the onions until translucent, about 8 minutes.

Combine ground pork and chopped bacon in a large bowl. Using fork and fingertips, mix together until well blended.

Add the onions, garlic, salt, thyme, anise seed, all spice, and pepper to the mixture and mix well. Add eggs, cream and reduced brandy. Stir until well blended.

Line 9 × 5 × 3 inch pan with bacon slices. Fill with pate mixture and fold the bacon strips over the top to cover the pate mix. Cover pan tightly with foil.

Bake in a water bath until center reaches 155°F, about 2½ hours.

Before removing the loaf pan from the water bath, use tin cans to weight the top of the pate. Chill overnight.

DUCK PROSCUITTO

- 2-1 lb boneless Moulard duck breasts with skin on
- 1½ cups kosher salt
- 1 cup (packed) dark brown sugar
- 5 juniper berries, cracked
- 3 bay leaves, crumbled
- 1 tsp coarsely cracked black pepper
- ¼ tsp smoked paprika

Using a small knife, trim all but a ⅛ inches layer of fat from each duck breast; reserve fat for rendering. Mix remaining ingredients in a medium bowl.

Arrange 2 sheets of plastic wrap side by side on a work surface. Spread 1 scant cup salt mixture (do not pack) in center of each sheet, spreading mixture to match the size of the duck breasts. Top each with 1 duck breast, fat side down. Spread remaining salt mixture over meat, dividing equally. Bring plastic wrap up and over each duck breast, wrapping tightly. Place on a small rimmed baking sheet, fat side down, and refrigerate for 7 days to cure.

Unwrap duck breasts. Scrape off salt mixture (do not rinse). Using a long, sharp knife, thinly slice meat.

CURED PORK TENDERLOIN (HAM)

- 1 cup kosher salt
- 1 cup sugar
- 12 cups boiling water
- 1 tsp black peppercorns
- 1 tsp mustard seeds
- ½ tsp allspice berries
- ½ tsp cloves
- ½ tsp dried thyme
- 2 bay leaves
- 1 tsp curing salt
- 1 cup dry white wine for brine, plus ½ cup for cooking
- 4 pork tenderloins, about 1 lb each
- 2 medium onions, thinly sliced
- 1 small bunch fresh thyme

Put salt and sugar in a large nonreactive bowl (stainless steel or glass). Add boiling water and stir well to dissolve salt and sugar. Add peppercorns, mustard seeds, allspice berries, cloves, thyme and bay leaves. Leave to cool completely.

Add curing salt and 1 cup white wine to cooled brine. Submerge pork tenderloins in brine. Place plate directly on top of pork to keep it submerged if necessary. Cover container and refrigerate for 5 days.

Remove pork from brine and pat dry. Discard brine. Spread onions and thyme sprigs on bottom of a large shallow baking dish. Add brined tenderloins in one layer, then add ½ cup wine. Heat oven to 350°F. As it heats, bring meat to room temperature. Cover dish and bake for 45 minutes or until pork registers 135°F with an instant-read thermometer. Remove from oven (meat will continue to cook and reach 140°F as it rests). Let cool before cutting into thin slices. Serve with buttermilk biscuits. Maybe refrigerated, well wrapped, for up to 1 week.

SAUSAGE FOR CHARCUTERIE

- 2 lbs pork shoulder – skinless, boneless
- 1 lbs pancetta
- 1½ tbsp dried oregano
- 1½ tbsp kosher salt
- 1 tbsp black pepper
- 1 tbsp red chili flakes
- 1 tbsp fennel seeds
- ¼ cup white wine
- 3 ft hog casing – well rinsed

Chill a large bowl along with the meat grinder and sausage stuffer attachments.

Fit the meat grinder with the largest die and grind the pork and pancetta, catching them in the chilled bowl. Add the salt, pepper, chili flakes, fennel seeds and wine.

Using your hands, combine thoroughly as quickly as possible.

Using the sausage stuffer, fill the casings with the meat and tie them in 8 inch links. Prick the sausages with a sterilized pin, arrange on a wire rack set over a baking sheet, and refrigerate, uncovered, overnight to allow the casings to relax.

Preheat convection oven to 250°F. Transfer the sausages to a clean baking rack.

Roast the sausages to an internal temperature of 150°F or until juices from the sausages run clear. Remove from the oven and allow to cool completely. Tie butcher's twine to the sausages and hang in the refrigerator two days until completely dried out and firm.

RED ONION BALSAMIC JAM

makes 2 cups

- 4 tbsp canola oil
- 4 medium red onions – thinly sliced
- 4 cups dry red wine
- ¾ cup brown sugar
- 6 tbsp red wine vinegar
- 6 tbsp balsamic vinegar
- Salt and pepper to taste

In a medium saucepan, heat the canola oil over medium-low. Sweat the onions, stirring occasionally, until they are softened without browning about 10 minutes.

Add the wine, brown sugar, red wine and balsamic vinegars, and continue cooking until the cooking liquid is thick, syrupy and almost totally reduced away, about 30 minutes. Season with salt and pepper. Serve warm or at room temperature.

GRAINY MUSTARD BLACK OLIVE TAPENADE

- 20 Kalamata olives – pits removed
- 1 tbsp capers
- ½ tbsp chopped garlic
- 2 tbsp grainy mustard
- 1 tsp lemon juice
- 2 tsp olive oil
- Cracked black pepper – lots if you love it!!

Add everything to a food processor and purée until smooth.

BREAD AND BUTTER PICKLES

- 3½ lbs pickling cucumbers
- ¾ lb onions
- 1 cup kosher salt
- Ice cubes
- 4 cups cider vinegar
- 2 cups water
- 4½ cups sugar
- 2 tbsp kosher or sea salt
- 3 tbsp yellow mustard seeds
- 2 tbsp celery seeds
- 1 tbsp dill seeds
- 1 tbsp coriander seeds
- 3 pcs star anise
- 1 tbsp white peppercorns
- ½ tsp tumeric
- 1-2 bay leaves

Slice the cucumbers ¼ inch thick. Cut the onions into thin wedges and separate them. Put the cucumbers and onions in a large bowl or stainless steel pot. Sprinkle 1 cup of salt over the onions and cucumbers, cover with ice, and let sit for 6 to 8 hours. Rinse well in a colander with cold water to wash away the salt brine.

Put the remaining ingredients in a stainless steel pot and bring to a boil. Place the pickles and onions in a large bowl or pot and pour the hot liquid over them. Stir well. Weight the pickles down with a plate to insure they are all submerged in the liquid. Let the pickles sit for 24 hours in the refrigerator before using.

8 6 oz portions beef tenderloin

8 tsp Pines Steak Rub (see Recipe Appendix page 123)

8 slices of smoked Atlantic salmon

24 asparagus spears – cut in 5 inch lengths and blanched quickly in boiling salted water

2 cups broccoli flowers – blanched in boiling salted water*

2 tbsp butter

1 cup aged white cheddar petals

2 cups Shiitake Mushroom Hollandaise

Salt and pepper

Grilled Alberta Beef Tenderloin and Smoked Salmon Wrapped Asparagus Spears

BROCCOLI FLOWERS, AGED WHITE CHEDDAR,
SHIITAKE MUSHROOM HOLLANDAISE SAUCE

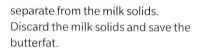

There is not a lot of beef main courses in this cookbook because we live on the east coast of Canada where seafood and scallops are KING!!

Serves 8

Serve this with your favourite potato or starch or a nice light salad.

Turn the BBQ grill on high heat. Spread ½ tsp of steak rub on both surfaces of the beef tenderloins.

Lay the slices of smoked salmon on a flat surface. Arrange three asparagus spears on the smoked salmon slice and roll the salmon around the asparagus. Season with salt and pepper and warm the smoked salmon / asparagus bundles in the oven to cook the smoked salmon.

Refresh the broccoli flowers in hot water and toss in butter, salt and pepper.

BBQ the tenderloins to preferred doneness. Place the tenderloin in the center of the plate and lean the smoked salmon asparagus against the meat. Place the buttered broccoli flowers around plate in a random manner. Spoon the shiitake mushroom hollandaise over the smoked salmon and the beef tenderloin. Top with some of the aged white cheddar petals.

*Blanching is the cooking process of boiling salted water and cooking vegetables about 50 to 60% of the way through, then quickly cooled in ice water.

PINES STEAK RUB
See Recipe Appendix page 123

SHIITAKE MUSHROOM HOLLANDAISE

- 1 **cup shiitake mushroom – stems removed; and cut in thin strips**
- 2 **tbsp butter**
- **Salt and pepper**

Hollandaise Sauce

- 2 **egg yolks**
- ¼ **cup reduction**
- 1 **lb butter – clarified**
- **Salt and pepper**

For the reduction

- 1 **cup white wine**
- **Juice from ½ lemon**
- ¼ **cup white vinegar**
- 1 **bay leaf**
- ½ **tsp black peppercorns**
- 1 **tbsp diced white onion**

Sautée the mushrooms in the butter and season with salt and pepper. Set aside.

TO CLARIFY BUTTER: Set the butter in a bowl over a warm area and allow it to melt. The butterfat will eventually separate from the milk solids. Discard the milk solids and save the butterfat.

FOR THE REDUCTION: In a small saucepan, bring all ingredients to a boil and reduce until less than a ¼ cup of liquid remains. Strain the reduction into a medium size stainless steel bowl.

Add the two egg yolks to the reduction and, over a double boiler on a medium heat, whisk the yolks with the reduction until the eggs are cooked to a thick ribbon stage. Be careful the water of the double boiler is not too hot as it will scramble your eggs and you will have to start again. When the eggs are cooked to a rich ribbon stage, remove from the heat and slowly whisk in the clarified butter. The hollandaise will multiply in volume to a light creamy yellow color. Season with salt and pepper and ladle over the poached eggs. Stir in the cooked shiitake mushrooms.

Grilled Medallions of Pork Tenderloin

APPLE ONION SAGE FRITTERS,
FRICASSÉE OF MUSHROOMS,
EGGPLANT AND SUNDRIED TOMATOES,
GRILLED STONE FRUIT CHUTNEY,
GRAINY MUSTARD SAUCE

Pork is so versatile and still relatively economical to purchase. It is one of the proteins that a chef utilises "nose-to-tail", to reduce the footprint and increase the variety of menu selections.

Serves 8

4 whole pork tenderloins – cleaned of all membrane
Pines Steak Rub (see Recipe Appendix page 123)
Apple Onion Sage Fritters
Fricassée of Mushrooms, Eggplant and Sundried Tomatoes
Grainy Mustard Sauce
Grilled Stone Fruit Churney (see Recipe Appendix page 121)

Turn the BBQ or grill to a medium high heat.

Cut the pork tenderloins into four equal pieces. Stand the pieces on their ends between two sheets of plastic wrap. With a meat mallet, gently punch down the tenderloin to about ¼ inch thickness. Season with some of the Pines Steak Rub and grill the pork tenderloin to preferred doneness.

APPLE ONION SAGE FRITTERS

2 Fuji apples – peeled, diced small, set aside
2 tbsp butter
1 medium onion, finely chopped
½ tsp dry mustard
¼ tsp paprika
2 tbsp fresh sage – chopped
    splash of bourbon
½ cup milk
1 egg
½ cup flour
1 tsp baking powder
½ tsp salt
    Butter
    Salt and pepper to taste

In a medium sauce pan melt the butter over medium-high heat and add the onion, seasoning with salt and pepper. Add the apple, mustard, paprika, sage and cook until they just barely begin to color. Pour in a splash of the bourbon, cook until the liquid is gone and remove from the heat. Set aside to cool.

Beat the egg into the milk until thoroughly combined. Combine the flour, baking powder and salt and add them to the milk and egg, stirring to form a batter.

When the apples and onions are cool enough (lukewarm will do it) fold them into the batter and mix until combined.

Melt some more butter (if you want to use oil at this point, that's cool — there's a decent amount of butter in there already) over medium-high heat, drop wads of the batter into the pan. Cook, flipping once or twice, until both sides are golden brown. Continue until the batter is all used up.

A sprinkling of kosher salt before serving wouldn't hurt.

FRICASSÉE OF MUSHROOMS, EGGPLANT AND SUNDRIED TOMATOES

4 tbsp butter
2 large onions – chopped in ½ inch pieces
2 cups whole white mushrooms
1 cup eggplant – cut in ½ inch cubes
¾ cup sundried tomatoes – cut in ½ inch pieces
1 tbsp summer savory
3 tbsp rice flour
2 cups chicken stock

In a large sauce pan or Dutch oven, melt the butter and fry the onions 6 to 7 minutes until translucent. Add the eggplant and fry until the eggplant browned and cooked through. Add in the sundried tomatoes and the summer savory. Dust the mixture with the rice flour and mix well to create a savory roux. Slowly add the chicken stock, stirring constantly to avoid clumping. Result will be a stew-like consistency. Turn down to a simmer and cook 30 minutes to gel flavors.

GRAINY MUSTARD SAUCE

- **1 oz canola oil**
- **½ cup onions – diced small**
- **1 cup red wine**
- **2 cup beef stock**
- **1 cup beef demi-glace**
- **2 tbsp grainy mustard**

In a medium saucepan, saute the onions in the canola oil. Add the red wine and reduce the volume by half. Add in the beef stock and continue to reduce, each time taking the volume down by half. Add the demi-glace and the grainy mustard and reduce until the sauce begins to thicken slightly. The flavors will become stronger as the volume reduces. Poor over and around the finished pork tenderloin.

GRILLED STONE FRUIT CHUTNEY
See Recipe Appendix page 121

PINES STEAK RUB
See Recipe Appendix page 123

Roast Rack of Nova Scotia Lamb

CURRIED SWEET POTATOES, ROASTED PARSNIPS,
SWEET N' HOT APRICOT CONDIMENT

When we think of lamb, we quickly think of New Zealand and Australia. Nova Scotia producers raise beautiful lamb which are larger in size, have a beautiful subtle lamb flavor and is easy to work with. The days of strong flavored mutton bathed in mint sauce are a thing of the past, and chefs work very hard to match new and exciting flavors with their Nova Scotia lamb.

Serves 6

2 Nova Scotia lamb racks – trimmed and bones scraped

1 tsp fresh thyme – chopped

1 tsp fresh rosemary – chopped

1 tsp fresh sage – chopped

2 tsp garlic – peeled and chopped

1 tbsp black peppercorns – fresh cracked

   Salt

¼ cup canola oil

3 tbsp honey

2 tbsp Dijon mustard

1 cup Panko bread crumbs

¼ cup butter – melted

4 medium size parsnips – skin on, washed, and cut on a bias ¼ inch thick

8 tbsp Sweet n' Hot Apricot Condiment

   Curried Sweet Potatoes

PREPARING THE LAMB: Set the oven to 300°F. Prepare an herb rub by mixing together the thyme, rosemary, sage, garlic, black pepper ad canola oil. Brush the lamb rack with the herb rub, season lightly with salt and sear all sides in a fry pan on medium high heat. Set aside.

Mix the honey, Dijon together. Mix together the panko bread crumbs and melted butter. When the lamb is at room temp, brush the surface of the lamb with the honey Dijon mixture and press the panko bread crumbs onto the surface.

Bake the lamb in the oven for approximately 25 to 30 minutes or until a meat thermometer registers 130°F. Remove from the oven and allow the lamb rack to rest for a few minutes before cutting. The center of the lamb should be a solid medium pink edge to edge.

ROAST PARSNIPS: Toss the sliced parsnips in a little canola oil, salt and pepper.

Spread them out on a sheet pan and roast along with the sweet potatoes at 400°F for about 15 to 20 minutes.

SWEET N' HOT APRICOT CONDIMENT

1½ pounds fresh apricots, chopped

½ cup red pepper – diced

1 small jalapeno – seeded and diced small

1½ cups sugar

1 tbsp fresh lemon juice

1 tbsp parsley – chopped

   Pinch salt

In medium saucepan, bring all ingredients to boil, lower heat and simmer until jamlike, about 25 minutes. Let cool, transfer to airtight container and refrigerate.

CURRIED SWEET POTATOES

2 sweet potatoes – skin on, cut in ½ inch disks

2 tbsp curry powder

4 tbsp Nova Scotia honey

3 tbsp canola oil

   Salt and pepper

Set oven to 400°F. Toss the sweet potatoes with the curry powder, the honey and the canola oil. Season with salt and pepper.

Place the sweet potato discs on a baking sheet. Do not use parchment because to achieve good caramelization, the potatoes need to be in contact with the baking sheet metal. Bake in the oven for 10 minutes. Turn the potatoes over and cook for another 10 to 15 minutes, or until the center of the potato is soft to the touch.

These potatoes keep well refrigerated for 3 or 4 days, but are usually gone before then. To reheat, use a microwave or warm in the oven.

Penne Noodles with Beef Tenderloin Tips

ROASTED BRUSSELS SPROUTS, GRILLED PEPPERS,
GREEN PEPPERCORNS, CREAM

It is hard to determine how guests think when they are deciding what to order. There is a nice balance of tastes and textures here with some big bold flavours. It is perhaps, not the healthiest pasta you will eat this week, but perhaps the most satisfying. Recommend to only make two pasta dishes in one pan for portioning purposes.

Serves 8

8 cups penne noodles – cooked

8 tbsp canola oil

24 oz. (3oz.each) beef tenderloin tips – cut in small pieces

2 cups Brussels sprouts – outer leaves removed, stem trimmed and blanched

1 red and 1 yellow pepper – cut in half, seeds and stems removed

8 tbsp green peppercorns – strained and crushed

4 cups 35% cream

Blanch the Brussels sprouts. Cut the sprouts in half, toss in a little oil, salt and pepper, and roast in the oven. Hold aside for your pasta dish.

Cut peppers in smaller pieces, toss in a little oil, salt and pepper, and grill. Cool and hold for later.

FOR 2 SERVIINGS: In a medium size saucepan, heat 2 tbsp canola oil until almost smoking. Add the beef tenderloin and stir fry. Season with salt and pepper. Add in ½ cup of Brussels sprouts and 4 tbsp of the grilled peppers and stir for a minute or so. Add one tbsp of the green peppercorns and one cup of the 35% cream.

Bring the mixture to a boil and cook until the cream begins to thicken. Add in two cups of penne noodles and stir to incorporate. Adjust seasoning with salt and pepper.

TIP: Best enjoyed with some great crusty grilled garlic bread.

THINGS WITH WINGS

Classic Club House

PESTO MAYO, CANADIAN CHEDDAR, ROAST
CHICKEN, BACON, TOASTED WHOLE WHEAT BREAD

The most popular sandwich on the planet!! We roast
fresh chickens for our clubs but it is the pesto mayo
that puts it over the top.

Serves 8

16 slices of Texas Style thick cut whole wheat bread – toasted
1½ cups Pesto Mayo
24 bacon rashers – pre-cooked
 8 slices real Canadian cheddar
24 oz sliced chicken breast – 3 oz per sandwich
16 slices tomato
 8 leaves of green leaf lettuce

Toast the slices of whole wheat bread. Lay three slices of bread
side by side.

Spread a tablespoon of Pesto Mayo on each slice of bread. Heat the bacon
and put three rashers of warm bacon on the left-hand slice of toast. Cover
the bacon with one slice of cheddar cheese. Warm the chicken, and on the
centre slice of toast, spread 3 oz of sliced chicken. Cover with two slices
of tomato and a leaf of lettuce. Lift the centre slice of toast onto the left-
hand slice of toast, and invert the right-hand slice and place on top of the
sandwich to finish it off.

Using long toothpicks to stabilize the club, slice the sandwich into four
quarters. Be careful not to apply too much pressure on the sandwich so
you finish with a mile-high clubhouse.

PESTO MAYO

easiest recipe ever

makes 2 cups

 2 **cups mayonnaise**
 3 **tbsp bottled pesto**
    Salt and pepper

Mix together in a stainless-steel bowl
and mix well. Season with salt and
pepper.

BBQ Pulled Chicken on Cheesy Corn Bread

JALAPENO HAVARTI CHEESE, MANGO CHIPOTLE CATSUP

Chicken does not need to be roasted an extreme length of time to become tender enough to pull apart into thin strips.

Serves 4

2 lb chicken
  Roast Chicken Rub
1 cup Minnie and Bo BBQ Sauce (see Recipe Appendix page 120)
2 slices of Cheesy Corn Bread
  softened butter
4 tbsp Mango Chipotle Catsup (See Recipe Appendix page 120)
1 slice jalapeno havarti cheese

Set the oven to 400°F.

Season the chicken with about 2 tbsp of chicken rub and sprinkle with salt and pepper. Roast the chicken for half an hour at 400°F. Turn the oven down to 250°F and cook for 1½ hours longer, or long enough so that the meat is ready to fall off the bone.

Transfer the chicken to a sheet pan and allow the chicken to rest and cool slightly. Using two forks, pull all the meat off the chicken and save the bones to make chicken stock. Continue to pull the chicken apart into thin strips.

While the chicken is warm, add 1 cup of BBQ sauce and 2 tbsp of chicken rub and mix it in.

THE FUN PART: Butter and grill two pieces of corn bread. On one slice, spread with some mango chipotle catsup, cover with a nice amount of warm pulled chicken and jalapeno havarti cheese. Place the second slice of corn bread on top and enjoy. If you prefer, add some sliced tomato and lettuce.

CHEESY CORN BREAD

1 cup all-purpose flour
1 cup yellow cornmeal
2 tsp salt
½ tsp fresh cracked black pepper
½ tsp cayenne pepper
2 tbsp sugar
2 tsp baking soda
1 cup buttermilk
2 large eggs
⅔ cup grated Monterey Jack or cheddar cheese
1 tbsp lemon juice
2 tbsp unsalted butter – melted
1 cup frozen corn kernels or 2 ears fresh corn, peeled, blanched and kernels removed

Preheat the oven to 400°F. Grease a 9 × 4 × 3 inch baking pan

In a large bowl, combine the flour, cornmeal, salt, pepper, cayenne, sugar, and baking soda and mix very well.

In a separate bowl, combine the buttermilk, eggs, cheese, and lemon juice. Beat together lightly, and pour into the flour mixture. Mix a few strokes, then add the melted butter and corn kernels and stir just until combined. Be careful not to over beat the batter.

Pour the batter into the baking pan and bake until the top is well browned and a toothpick inserted in the center comes out clean, about 40 to 50 minutes.

ROAST CHICKEN RUB

1 cup Montreal steak spice
¼ cup curry powder
⅓ cup paprika
⅓ cup smoked paprika
½ cup dried thyme

Mix together, but season the chicken with salt and pepper before putting into the oven.

MINNIE AND BO BBQ SAUCE
See Recipe Appendix page 120

MANGO CHIPOTLE CATSUP
See Recipe Appendix page 120

The 100 Kilometre Experience

The 100 Kilometre Experience is an ever-evolving dish which relies on locally sourced product from the ground, air and sea within a 100 kilometre radius of the Digby Pines.

Fun fact: Our organic flour used occasionally in preparation, comes from the other side of the Bay of Fundy, just outside Saint John in New Brunswick, but still within the 100 kilometre radius.

The purpose of the 100 Kilometre Experience is to utilize locally sourced products within a short distance of our front door. Depending where you live, this may change things a little, but as one of our environmental initiatives, we focus on what we are certain comes from within the 100 kilometres of the Digby Pines. The dish evolves over the season, as small local growers are eager to have their fruits and vegetables show up on our menus. The 100 Kilometre Experience you enjoyed in May will look drastically different when September rolls around. Every chef's dream is to have farmers, growers and producers deliver the fruits of their labor, still warm out of the ground or off the tree, right to their back door.

Serves 8

8 large locally sourced chicken breasts – skin on
   Salt and pepper
   Ricotta and Spinach Dumplings
   Spiced Apples (see Recipe Appendix page 123)
   Pan Juices (see Recipe Appendix page 123)

Season the chicken breasts with salt and pepper. Pan sear to a golden brown and finish cooking in the oven.

HOME MADE RICOTTA CHEESE

makes 2 cups

2 **quarts whole milk,**

⅓ **cup lemon juice (from 1½ to 2 lemons), ⅓ cup distilled white vinegar, or ½ tsp citric acid (available from cheese-making suppliers)**

1 **tsp salt, optional**

Warm the milk to 200°F. Pour the milk into a 4-quart pot and set it over medium heat. Let it warm gradually to 200°F, monitoring the temperature with an instant read thermometer. The milk will get foamy and start to steam; remove it from heat if it starts to boil.

Add the lemon juice and salt: Remove the milk from heat. Pour in the lemon juice or vinegar (or citric acid) and the salt. Stir gently to combine.

Let the milk sit for 10 minutes: Let the pot of milk sit undisturbed for 10 minutes. After this time, the milk should have separated into clumps of milky white curds and thin, watery, yellow-colored whey — dip your slotted spoon into the mix to check. If you still see a lot of un-separated milk, add another tablespoon of lemon juice or vinegar and wait a few more minutes.

Strain the curds: Set a strainer over a bowl and line the strainer with cheese cloth. Scoop the big curds out of the pot with a slotted spoon and transfer them to the strainer. Pour the remaining curds and the whey through the strainer. (Removing the big curds first helps keep them from splashing and making a mess as you pour.)

Drain the curds for 10 to 60 minutes: Let the ricotta drain for 10 to 60 minutes, depending on how wet or dry you prefer your ricotta. If the ricotta becomes too dry, you can also stir some of the whey back in before using or storing it.

Use or store the ricotta: Fresh ricotta can be used right away or refrigerated in an airtight container for up to a week.

RICOTTA AND SPINACH DUMPLINGS

2 **cups homemade ricotta cheese (see recipe for Home Made Ricotta Cheese, opposite page)**

4 **cups local spinach – blanched, shocked, drained, squeezed and chopped**

1 **egg**

1 **cup Spearville all-purpose organic flour**

Salt and pepper

In a large stainless-steel bowl, combine the ricotta cheese, chopped spinach and the egg. Mix to combine.

Add half of the flour and fold together with the cheese mixture. Add some salt and pepper. Add the remaining flour, once again folding to combine. If the dough is too wet, add a bit more flour. Add just enough flour so that the dough stays together but is still light and fluffy.

In a medium saucepan, bring water to a boil and turn it down to a simmer temperature. Using two teaspoons, scoop and shape the ricotta mixture into little dumplings and poach until firm. Remove the dumplings from the poaching liquid and reserve on an oiled sheet pan. Let cool.

Fry the dumplings to a light brown in a non-stick fry pan.

SPICED APPLES
See Recipe Appendix page 122

PAN JUICES
See Recipe Appendix page 123

Buttermilk Fried Crispy Quail

SOUR APPLE VANILLA COMPOTE, POLENTA FRIES,
MAPLE GASTRIQUE

Serves 8

- 8 quail (16 halves) – boneless
- 2 cups buttermilk
- 2 tbsp Italian seasoning, or ⅓ cup of mixed chopped fresh herbs like oregano, thyme and parsley
- 2 tsp paprika
- 1 tbsp garlic powder
- 1 tsp cayenne pepper
- 2 cups flour
- 1 tbsp salt
- 3 cups vegetable oil
  Maple Gastrique
  Sour Apple Vanilla Compote
  Polenta Fries

Mix the buttermilk with all the spices (except the salt). Coat the quail and set in a covered container for a least an hour, and as much as 4 hours. When you are ready to fry, pour the oil into a large pan and heat at medium high heat. The oil should be deep enough to submerge the quail. Meanwhile, take the quail out of the buttermilk and let it drain in a colander. Don't shake off the buttermilk. Let the oil heat to 325°F, this is the point where a sprinkle of flour will immediately sizzle. Do not let the oil smoke! Fry for about 4 to 5 minutes. A counter top deep fryer set at 350°F is an option.

MAPLE GASTRIQUE

- 1 cup maple syrup
- ½ cup red wine vinegar
- ½ piece cinnamon stick
- 1 piece star anise
- 1 cup apple juice

Combine and simmer slowly until mixture returns to a syrup consistency.

SOUR APPLE VANILLA COMPOTE

- 2 cups water
- ⅓ cup sugar
- ½ vanilla bean – split in half
- 1 tbsp Calvados or brandy
- ½ tsp ground cinnamon
- ⅛ tsp ground cloves
- ⅛ tsp ground nutmeg
  Pinch salt
- 8 golden delicious apples (large, peeled, cored and cubed)

In a large stock pot, add the water and sugar and heat until the sugar is dissolved. Add the vanilla bean, calvados, cinnamon, cloves, nutmeg and salt. Simmer for 15 minutes.

Add the apples and turn heat to medium. Cook until the apples are soft. Strain the apples and mash to remove most of the lumps. Add the stock back in until a pourable, spreadable consistency is achieved. Taste and adjust seasoning.

POLENTA FRIES

- 2 cups milk
- ¾ cup cornmeal
- ¼ cup parmesan cheese
- 2 egg yolks
- 1 tbsp fresh basil – finely chopped
  Salt and pepper

Bring milk to a boil. Slowly add the cornmeal while whisking the milk. Reduce the heat to medium. Using a wooden spoon continue to stir the polenta for 15 minutes. Add the egg yolks, parmesan cheese and chopped basil. Continue to stir for five minutes on low heat. The polenta will pull away from the sides of the pot and will be very hard to stir.

Spread the polenta onto a small greased baking pan until it's an even ½ inch thick. Cool in the fridge. Cut the polenta into even fries, ½ × ½ × 3 inches. Deep fry in hot oil for approximately 4 minutes or until polenta is golden brown.

Molasses BBQ Cornish Game Hen

APPLE JUNIPER BRAISED PURPLE CABBAGE, BUTTERMILK AMERICAN
POPOVERS, ROASTED BRUSSELS SPROUTS, MINNIE AND BO BBQ SAUCE

Cornish game hen is one of the fun foods to eat. If the birds are small enough, serve a whole bird, if not, a half is enough to satisfy a craving. The molasses in the Minnie and Bo BBQ sauce gives the sauce an added dimension of flavour.

Serves 8

4   game hens – bones removed. If you do not have the ability to de-bone the game hens, simply brush the molasses BBQ sauce on whole game hens and roast accordingly.

3   cups Molasses BBQ Sauce

4   cups Apple Juniper Braised Purple Cabbage

16   pcs Buttermilk American Popovers

32   pcs Brussels sprouts – stem trimmed, cut in half, tossed in canola oil, salt and pepper. Roast at 350°F, turning occasionally, until soft in the center.

Preheat oven to 350°F.

Brush the game hens with the molasses BBQ sauce, salt and pepper, and mark it on the BBQ grill. Remove to a roasting pan and finish the roasting in the oven. If the hens are boneless, they will roast quicker than the whole bone-in version.

In a medium fry pan, heat the apple juniper braised purple cabbage and build a little pile in the center of the plate. Put the popovers in the oven to re-heat and place two pieces per plate. Scatter the Brussels sprouts around the plate.

When the hens are cooked, simply cut them in half and lay them on the plate.

BUTTERMILK AMERICAN POPOVERS

15   fluid oz buttermilk

½   tsp salt

2   tbsp butter – melted

5   eggs – lightly beaten

8   oz all-purpose flour – sifted

Preheat the oven to 425°F. Combine the buttermilk, salt, butter and eggs in a mixing bowl. Add the flour and beat until smooth. The batter should have the consistency of thick cream.

Butter a 12-hole deep bun tray (muffin tin) and half fill the hollows with the batter. Bake in the preheated oven for 15 minutes, then reduce the temperature to 375°F and bake for 15 to 20 minutes longer, or until the popovers are well risen and golden brown.

MOLASSES BBQ SAUCE

Mix 1 cup of molasses into 2 cups of Minnie and Bo BBQ Sauce (see recipe appendix page 120). Use to brush on the game hens and to baste with while cooking.

APPLE JUNIPER BRAISED PURPLE CABBAGE

1   garlic clove – smashed

3   tbsp butter

2   lb red cabbage – cored and cut into ½-inch strips

1   gala or Fuji apple – cored and cut into ½-inch pieces to match cabbage

½   cup apple cider OR apple juice

1   tsp juniper berries

½   tsp caraway seeds

1½   tbsp apple cider vinegar

Cook garlic in butter in a 12 inch heavy skillet over medium heat, stirring, 1 minute. Add cabbage, apple, apple cider (or apple juice), juniper berries, caraway, 1 tsp salt, and ½ tsp pepper and cook, covered, stirring occasionally, until cabbage is tender, 15 to 18 minutes. Add vinegar and cook, uncovered, stirring occasionally, until liquid has evaporated, 2 to 3 minutes. Season with salt and pepper.

Duck Confit Spring Rolls

PICKLED NAPA CABBAGE, ASIAN LIME GLAZE

Who doesn't love light crispy spring rolls. The contrast of crispy with the soft and crunchy fillings stimulates the senses. A sharp sweet n' sour glaze only lends more contrast to the experience.

Serves 8

16 8 inch spring roll wrappers

1 egg – for egg wash

Oil for frying

SPRING ROLL FILLING

2 cups Duck Confit (see Recipe Appendix page 123)

1 tbsp canola oil

2 carrots – shredded

2 green onions – cut in thin strips

4 cups green cabbage – shredded

½ cup red onion – thinly sliced strips

4 tbsp mirin (sweet cooking rice wine)

2 tbsp soya sauce

2 tbsp honey

1 tbsp lime juice

2 tbsp grated ginger

TO SERVE

Asian Honey Lime Soya Glaze

Pickled Napa Cabbage Slaw (see Recipe Appendix page 121)

Heat the 1 tbsp of oil in a large pot. Add the carrots, onions and red onions, and cook for five minutes on medium heat. Add the cabbage and remainder of ingredients. Cook until cabbage is reduced and limp, approximately 10 to 15 minutes. Fold in the duck confit and allow to cool before stuffing spring rolls.

TO FILL THE SPRING ROLLS: Place the spring roll wrappers on a flat surface with the corners forward and away. Spoon about 2 ounces of confit filling onto the wrapper and spread it out lengthwise across the wrapper. Fold the bottom half of the wrapper over the filling, but not all the way to the top. Gently tuck the wrapper back against the filling and then proceed to fold the ends over into the center of the spring roll. While applying a bit of pressure, roll towards the top creating a nice tight spring roll. Before finishing the roll, egg wash the top to create a solid seal so the spring roll doesn't come undone in the fryer.

FRY THE SPRING ROLLS: fry at 350°F in a deep fryer, or very hot oil in a fry pan on the stove rolling the spring roll (a bit more tricky) to brown on all sides.

ASIAN HONEY LIME SOYA GLAZE

2 cloves garlic – minced

1 tbsp fresh ginger – grated

1 tbsp vegetable oil

2 tbsp coriander seeds

2 tbsp fennel seeds

4 star anise

2 cups honey

½ cup lime juice – fresh or Realime Juice

1 cup soy sauce

1 cup sake or white table wine

1 cup brown sugar

½ cup orange juice

2 tbsp rice wine vinegar

1 tsp sambal olek

Toast coriander seeds, fennel seeds and start anise for 3 minutes.

Gently fry the garlic and ginger in the vegetable oil 3 to 5 minutes. Do not brown.

Add the remaining ingredients and simmer until syrupy, about 1 hour.

DUCK CONFIT

See Recipe Appendix page 123

PICKLED NAPA CABBAGE SLAW

See Recipe Appendix 121

Perogies Filled with Confit of Duck

RHUBARB CHUTNEY, BLOOD ORANGE SWIRL, WILTED BEET GREENS

The tartness of the rhubarb chutney and the blood orange will soften the richness of the duck perogies. The wilted beet greens provide another texture and make sure you eat some vegetable today.

Serves 8

3½ cups all-purpose flour

3 large eggs

2 tbsp sour cream

1 cup water; more if needed

Butter or vegetable oil

Salt and pepper

Duck Confit (see Recipe Appendix page 123)

Sweet n' Tart Rhubarb Chutney

Blood Orange Purée

MAKE THE DOUGH: In a large bowl, combine the flour, eggs, sour cream and ½ of the water. Stir, beating the eggs as you mix. Gradually add the rest of the water, stirring until the mixture begins to come together. Turn the dough onto a well-floured surface. Knead gently with your fingertips, lifting the dough off the counter and dropping it down (the dropping technique is key for delicate and pliable dough), taking care not to overwork it. Knead until the ingredients are blended and the dough is smooth on the outside and slightly sticky when poked with finger tips, 2 to 5 minutes. Gather in a ball, wrap in plastic, and let rest for at least 20 minutes.

Roll the dough to a thickness of ¼ inch. Using a 2 inch round cutter, cut as many rounds as you can.

STUFFING AND FRYING THE PEROGIES:
After cutting the perogie dough into rounds, place a round of dough in the palm of your hand. Scoop an appropriate amount of duck confit into the center of the dough. Damp the edges with the water and close your hand to form a half moon. Squeeze the edges tight to seal the perogie. Continue until all the filling is used or all the dough is gone.

Bring a Dutch oven of water to a boil over high heat; add the perogies in batches. Reduce heat to a gentle simmer; cook for 1 to 2 minutes or until perogies float to the surface and are tender. Remove with a slotted spoon and cool on a baking sheet sprayed with non-stick spray.

Melt some butter in a frypan and add some onions. Add in six perogies and fry to light browning on the onions and perogies.

SWEET N' TART RHUBARB CHUTNEY

1 lb rhubarb – cut in half to ½ inch sections

5 tbsp granulated sugar

Juice from one lemon

¼ cup water

Add all the ingredients to a medium sauce pan and bring to a boil. Reduce the heat and simmer until the rhubarb has broken down to a stew consistency.

Remove from the heat and cool. Refrigerate until ready to use.

BLOOD ORANGE PURÉE

3 blood oranges – peeled and all pith removed; coarsely chopped

½ cup brown sugar

2 tsp cornstarch

Put all ingredients in a small sauce pan and bring to a boil. Stir occasionally. Turn down to a simmer and cook until the pulp all renders out and the juice thickens about 10 minutes.

Press the blood oranges through a strainer and cool completely.

WILTED BEET GREENS

8 cups beet greens – heavier part of the stems removed and chopped

½ cup water

1 tbsp butter

Salt and pepper

In a medium size sauce pot, add the water and the chopped beet greens. The beet greens will cook and reduce in volume. Cool the greens in cold water.

In a fry pan, melt the butter and add the wilted beet greens. Season with salt and pepper and stir to incorporate.

DUCK CONFIT

See Recipe Appendix page 123

Spaghettini in Olive Oil with Roast Chicken

GOAT CHEESE, SUN-DRIED TOMATOES, CARAMELIZED ONIONS

This pasta is a light alternative to the heavier noodles like fettuccini. The Mediterranean flavors are fresh and they work really well together. Goat cheese should be declared a food group!!

Serves 8

- ¼ cup extra virgin olive oil
- 2 lbs (3 oz per serving) roast chicken – shredded
- ½ cup good quality sun-dried tomatoes – cut in julienne
- 8 cups spaghettini – cooked
- 1 lb goat cheese – 2 oz per serving
- 4 medium onions – sliced in julienne
- 4 tsp canola oil – for caramelized onions
- Salt and pepper

CARAMELIZE THE ONIONS: Coat the bottom of the pan with olive oil, or a mixture of olive oil and butter (about 1 tsp per onion). Heat the pan on medium high heat until the oil is shimmering. Add the onion slices and stir to coat the onions with the oil. Spread the onions out evenly over the pan and let cook, stirring occasionally.

ROAST THE CHICKEN: Season the chicken with about 2 tablespoons of chicken rub and sprinkle with salt and pepper. Roast the chicken for half an hour at 400°F. Turn the oven down to 250°F and cook for 1½ hours longer, or long enough so that the meat is ready to fall off the bone.

Transfer the chicken to a sheet pan and allow the chicken to rest and cool slightly. Using two forks, pull all the meat off the chicken and save the bones to make chicken stock. Continue to pull the chicken apart into thin strips.

While the chicken is warm, add 1 cup of barbecue sauce and 2 tbsp of chicken rub and mix it in.

MAKE THE PASTA: In a large straight sided fry pan, heat the olive oil and saute the roasted chicken. Continue to stir the chicken and season with salt and pepper. Add in the sundried tomatoes and the caramelized onions. Finish by adding in the goat cheese and spaghettini noodles and stir and toss until all the ingredients are incorporated.

Portion the pasta into eight pasta bowls and garnish with extra caramelized onions and perhaps some additional goat cheese.

ROAST CHICKEN RUB

- 1 cup Montreal steak spice
- ¼ cup curry powder
- ⅓ cup paprika
- ⅓ cup smoked paprika
- ½ cup dried thyme

Mix together, but season the chicken with salt and pepper before putting into the oven.

FINAL TOUCHES

Almond Rice Pudding

NOVA SCOTIA BLUEBERRIES, PINOT NOIR SAUCE,
CANDIED ALMONDS

Serves 8 – 10

4 cups milk

¾ cup rice (white long grain or basmati)

½ cup sugar

½ tsp almond extract

½ cup almonds – sliced and toasted

6 tbsp sherry wine

2 cups 35% cream

Scald milk in a heavy saucepan. Add the rice and bring to a simmer over medium heat and cook 10 to 15 minutes. Reduce heat to low, cover pan and cook until all of the milk is absorbed. Stir in sugar, almond extract, almonds, sherry and chill.

Once rice is chilled, whip the cream until stiff peaks form and fold it into the rice mixture.

BLUEBERRY PINOT NOIR SAUCE

1 cup frozen blueberries

½ cup Pinot Noir

1 tbsp sugar or currant jelly

Place the blueberries in a small pot with the wine, ½ cup water and the sugar or jelly. Bring to a boil. Reduce the heat and simmer until the blueberries and juice is syrupy, approximately 20 minutes.

CANDIED ALMONDS

1½ cups whole almonds

3 tbsp sugar

¼ tsp salt

2 tbsp maple syrup

2 tsp water

1 tsp canola oil

1 tsp vanilla extract

½ tsp cinnamon

Preheat the oven to 350°F. Place a piece of parchment paper on a baking sheet and set aside. On another baking sheet, spread the almonds and bake for 7 to 12 minutes, stirring halfway, or until they smell toasted. Remove the almonds from the oven and set aside.

In a large bowl, combine the sugar with the salt and set aside. Combine the maple syrup, water, oil, vanilla and cinnamon in a medium saucepan over medium-high heat. Bring to a boil, reduce heat to medium, and add the almonds. Cook until almost all of the liquid has evaporated, stirring often; about 2 to 4 minutes. Remove the pan from the heat and transfer the nuts to the bowl with the sugar and toss until well coated.

Pour the almonds evenly onto the parchment-lined pan and cool completely. The nuts will be soft initially, but will become crunchy as they cool.

Triple Chocolate Terrine

STRAWBERRY RELISH, ORANGE CUSTARD SAUCE

Rich, dense, and super chocolatey, the term terrine denotes the shape of the mold this dessert is made in. It can also be made in a loaf pan if that is what you have at home.

Makes one 8 × 4 inch loaf

1	tbsp melted butter
18	oz bittersweet chocolate
½	cup unsalted butter
12	egg yolks
6	tbsp sugar – divided
3	egg whites
¾	cup 35% cream
2	tbsp sour cream

Butter a loaf pan with melted butter. Line the pan with parchment paper.

Melt the bittersweet chocolate and the butter in a pan over very low heat. Set aside. In a bowl, beat the egg yolks and 4 tbsp of the sugar until mousse-like in consistency. Fold ⅓ of the yolk mixture into chocolate mixture until combined. Then fold remaining yolk mixture into chocolate mixture. Return the mixture to a heat proof bowl. Whisk over a double boiler until a whisk run through the bowl leaves a trail (or slight trough) in the mixture. Remove from heat and set aside to cool.

In a separate bowl, whip the egg whites with 1 tbsp of the sugar until stiff. Fold ⅓ of the egg whites into the chocolate/egg mixture until combined. Then gently fold in the remaining egg whites.

In a separate bowl, whip the heavy cream and the sour cream with the remaining 1 tbsp of sugar until mousse-like in consistency. Fold ⅓ of the cream mixture into the chocolate/egg mixture just until combined. Then very gently fold the remaining cream mixture into the chocolate/egg mixture.

Pour the mixture into the lined loaf pan and refrigerate overnight.

ORANGE CUSTARD SAUCE

2	cups 35% cream
½	vanilla bean – split lengthwise, seed removed
4	egg yolks
⅓	cup sugar
3	tbsp orange juice
1	small orange – zested

In a saucepan, combine the cream with the vanilla bean and bring to a boil.

In a heat proof bowl, beat together the yolks with the sugar and orange juice until smooth.

Add in the orange zest. Pour the cream into the yolk/orange mixture and beat together.

Pour the mixture back into the saucepan and heat slowly, stirring constantly. When the mixture thickens enough to coat the back of a spoon. Remove from the heat, remove the vanilla bean (save, packed in sugar for later use) and cool over an ice bath stirring occasionally until cold.

STRAWBERRY RELISH

16	medium sized ripe strawberries
1	tbsp sugar
1	tbsp lemon juice

Hull the strawberries and cut them into a very small dice. Add the sugar and lemon juice and mix together. The sugar and lemon will draw out some of the strawberry juices. Reserve for plating.

Lemon Raspberry Tart with Hazelnut Crust

Raspberries and lemon are fresh and light and makes a wonderful summertime dessert. If nut allergies are an issue, just use a pie dough that does not involve nuts and the results will be just as delicious. These tarts can be made as one large raspberry tart, or several smaller individual desserts or even small bite size mini desserts.

Serves 8

HAZELNUT PIE DOUGH

- 1 cup hazelnuts – skin on
- 1 cup all-purpose flour
- 2 tbsp granulated sugar
- ¾ tsp salt
- ½ cup chilled unsalted butter – cut into pieces

Preheat oven to 350°F.

Toast hazelnuts on a baking sheet, 8 to 10 minutes; let cool. Using a kitchen towel, rub hazelnuts together to remove most of the skins. Some skins may cling but that is alright.

Pulse flour, sugar, salt, and the hazelnuts in a food processor until the consistency of coarse meal. Add butter to dry ingredients and pulse until there are only a few pea-size pieces of butter remaining.

Transfer mixture to a large bowl; drizzle 3 tbsp ice water over and mix, adding another splash or so of water if needed, just to bring dough together.

Using your fingers, press dough evenly 1½ to 2 inches up the sides and then into the bottom of pan; compact and smooth with a flat, straight-sided measuring cup or glass. Chill 20 minutes.

Bake crust until golden but not totally baked through, 15 to 20 minutes. Transfer to a wire rack and let cool 10 minutes.

LEMON CUSTARD

- 1 cup white sugar
- 2 tbsp all-purpose flour
- 3 tbsp cornstarch
- ¼ tsp salt
- 1½ cups water
- 2 lemons – juiced and zested
- 2 tbsp butter
- 4 egg yolks – beaten

In a medium saucepan, whisk together 1 cup sugar, flour, cornstarch, and salt. Stir in water, lemon juice and lemon zest. Cook over medium-high heat, stirring frequently, until mixture comes to a boil. Stir in butter. Place egg yolks in a small bowl and gradually whisk in ½ cup of hot sugar mixture. Whisk egg yolk mixture back into remaining sugar mixture.

Bring to a boil and continue to cook while stirring constantly until thick. Remove from heat. Pour filling into baked pastry shell.

When the custard is cool, line the top of the tart with raspberries. Before serving, dust with icing sugar.

RASPBERRY COULIS

- 1 cup frozen raspberries – thawed
- ¼ cup water
- 2 tbsp icing sugar

In a blender, purée the raspberries, water and icing sugar until smooth. Strain the purée through a fine sieve to separate the seeds.

CRÈME ANGLAISE

see Recipe Appendix page 120

Dome Royal 2016

BLUEBERRY MOUSSE, BLUEBERRY PATE,
CHOCOLATE GLAZE

We have had a "Dome" of some flavor since my time at the Digby Pines. It is always a popular dessert choice with mousse inside, berries and appropriate sauce to garnish.

Makes 8 to 10 Domes

TO ASSEMBLE THE DOME

Use 10 consistent size small bowls (large enough for a dessert portion) and line them with plastic wrap. Press the wrap tight to the bottom and around the edges of the bowl.

Fill the bowls half way with the blueberry mousse. Insert one of the discs of blueberry pate and press gently down into the mousse. Cover with another layer of the mousse, cover with plastic and freeze for two hours.

After two hours, turn out and unwrap the domes and place them on a wire rack. Warm the chocolate glaze until pliable and stir well but don't let it get too hot.

Using a large ladle, scoop and pour the chocolate glaze over the domes being sure to completely cover them. Once all covered, repeat the process and refrigerate right away. Using a narrow paint brush, paint a cross of blueberry coulis on the plate. Lay a finished dome on the center of the cross and garnish with berries and available fruit.

BLUEBERRY MOUSSE

- 1 lemon juice – fresh squeezed
- ⅔ cup icing sugar
- ½ vanilla bean – split and seeds scraped
- ¾ lb blueberries
- 1 tsp gelatin powder
- 2 egg whites
  Pinch of cream of tartar
- 3 oz 35% cream

Place the lemon juice, half of the icing sugar, the vanilla bean, scraped seeds and the blueberries in a small saucepan and bring to a simmer over low heat. Cook for 5 minutes, then remove from the heat. Transfer half the cooked blueberries to a bowl to cool. Place the remaining berries in a fine sieve placed over a bowl and press down to extract as much purée as possible. Discard the solids.

Whisk the gelatin into the warm purée until it has all melted, then refrigerate until cool but not set. Using electric beaters, whisk the egg whites and cream of tartar until stiff peaks form. Whisk in the remaining sugar until glossy and the sugar has dissolved.

Next, whisk the cream until soft peaks form, then fold into the cold blueberry purée. Gently fold in the beaten egg whites.

CHOCOLATE GLAZE

- 2 tbsp butter
- 2 oz unsweetened chocolate
- 1 cup icing sugar
- 2 tbsp water – boiling

Combine the butter and chocolate in a saucepan over low heat. Cook, stirring until melted.

Sift the icing sugar into a small bowl. Stir the sifted sugar into the melted butter and chocolate. Beat the mixture, adding boiling water until thinned as desired. If you happen to find it too thin, add a little more icing sugar. If too thick, add more hot water.

Drizzle the chocolate glaze over cake or use it as a cookie or brownie icing. It makes an excellent glaze for cream puffs, eclairs, or doughnuts.

If it stands too long, it will thicken. Just put it over the heat to thin it out again.

BLUEBERRY COULIS

To brush on the plate

- 1 cup frozen Nova Scotia wild blueberries
- 1 cup fresh Nova Scotia wild blueberries
- 4 tbsp icing sugar
- 1 tbsp lemon juice – fresh squeezed

Put all ingredients into a blender and purée until smooth. Pass through a fine sieve.

BLUEBERRY PATE

Yield: about 30 – ¼ inch thick discs

- 1 **lb Anjou pears**
- ½ **lb frozen blueberries**
- 2 **cups sugar – divided**
- ¼ **cup water**
- 1 **3oz package liquid pectin**
- 1½ **tbsp lemon juice – fresh squeezed**

Line an 8 inch square pan with aluminum foil, or use an 8 inch square disposable aluminum pan.

Wash the pears, peel them, slice them in half, and core them. In a medium saucepan over medium heat, stir together the pears, the blueberries, one cup of the sugar, and the water, and simmer gently until the pears are quite tender, about 20 minutes. Let the mixture cool slightly. Then purée it in a blender or food processor, in batches if necessary, until it is very smooth.

Return the purée to the pan and add the pectin, lemon juice and the remainder of the sugar. Bring to a low simmer and cook, stirring frequently, especially as it reduces, until the mixture is quite thick, about 45 minutes to one hour. It should part briefly when you run a wooden spoon down the middle. Scrape the purée into your pan and smooth the surface with a spatula. Let it cool at room temperature for an hour. Then cover it with cellophane and refrigerate it for two hours, or up to two weeks. Using a 1 inch round cutter, cut as many blueberry pate rounds as you can. Freeze what you don't need for later.

Opera Cake

JACONDE SPONGE, COFFEE BUTTERCREAM,
CHOCOLATE GANACHE

Celebrating the six acts of a popular opera, this cake is labor intensive but the effort is well worth it. The perfect finish to a great meal, this dessert is light and rich but not too filling.

TO ASSEMBLE THE CAKE

Prepare the Jaconde Sponge Cake, Coffee Syrup, Chocolate Ganache, Coffee Buttercream, and Chocolate Glaze.

Line a baking sheet with parchment or wax paper. Working with one sheet of cake at a time, trim the cake so that you have two pieces: one 10 × 10 inch square and one 10 × 5 inch rectangle. Place one square of cake on the parchment and moisten the layer with coffee syrup. Spread about three-quarters of the coffee buttercream evenly over the cake. (If the buttercream is soft, put the cake in the freezer for about 10 minutes before proceeding.) Top with the two rectangular pieces of cake, placing them side by side to form a square; moisten with syrup. Spread the ganache over the surface, top with the last cake layer, moisten, then chill the cake in the freezer for about 10 minutes. Cover the top of the cake with a thin layer of coffee buttercream. This is to smooth the top and ready it for the glaze. Refrigerate the cake for at least 1 hour or for up to 6 hours; it should be cold when you pour over the glaze. If you're in a hurry, pop the cake into the freezer for about 20 minutes, then continue.

Lift the chilled cake off the parchment-lined pan and place it on a rack. Put the rack over the parchment-lined pan and pour over the glaze, using a long offset spatula to help smooth it evenly across the top. Slide the cake into the refrigerator to set the glaze and chill the cake, which should be served slightly chilled. At serving time, use a long thin knife, dipped in hot water and wiped dry, to carefully trim the sides of the cake so that the drips of glaze are removed and the layers revealed.

JACONDE SPONGE CAKE

- 6 **large egg whites** – at room temperature
- 2 **tbsp granulated sugar**
- 2 **cups ground blanched almonds**
- 2¼ **cups icing sugar** – sifted
- 6 **large eggs**
- ½ **cup all-purpose flour**
- 3 **tbsp unsalted butter** – melted and cooled briefly

Position the oven racks to divide the oven into thirds and preheat the oven to 425°F. Line two 12½ × 15½ inch (31 × 39 cm) jelly-roll pans with parchment paper and brush with melted butter. (This is in addition to the quantity in the ingredient list.)

Working in a clean dry mixer bowl fitted with the whisk attachment, beat the egg whites until they form soft peaks. Add the granulated sugar and beat until the peaks are stiff and glossy. If you do not have another mixer bowl, gently scrape the whites into another bowl.

In a mixer fitted with the paddle attachment, beat the almonds, icing sugar and whole eggs on medium speed until light and voluminous, about 3 minutes. Add the flour and beat on low speed only until it disappears. Using a rubber spatula, gently fold the meringue into the almond mixture, then fold in the melted butter. Divide the batter between the pans and spread it evenly to cover the entire surface of each pan.

Bake the cakes for 5 to 7 minutes, or until they are lightly browned and just springy to the touch. Put the pans on a heatproof counter, cover each with a sheet of parchment or wax paper, turn the cakes over and unmold. Carefully peel away the parchment, turn the parchment over and use it to cover the exposed sides of the cakes. Let the cakes come to room temperature between the parchment or wax paper sheets. (The cakes can be made up to 1 day ahead, wrapped and kept at room temperature.)

COFFEE SYRUP

½ **cup water**

⅓ **cup sugar**

1½ **tbsp instant espresso or coffee**

Stir everything together in a small saucepan and bring to a boil. Cool. (The syrup can be covered and refrigerated for up to 1 week.)

CHOCOLATE GANACHE

8 **ounces bittersweet chocolate, finely chopped**

½ **cup whole milk**

¼ **cup heavy cream**

4 **tbsp unsalted butter, at room temperature**

Put the chocolate in a medium bowl and keep it close at hand. Bring the milk and cream to a full boil, pour it over the chocolate, wait 1 minute, then stir gently until the ganache is smooth and glossy.

Beat the butter until it is smooth and creamy, then stir it into the ganache in 2 to 3 additions. Refrigerate the ganache, stirring every 5 minutes, until it thickens and is spreadable, about 20 minutes. (The ganache can be packed airtight and refrigerated for up to 3 days or frozen for 1 month; bring to room temperature before using.)

COFFEE BUTTERCREAM

2 **tbsp instant espresso or coffee**

2 **tbsp boiling water**

1 **cup sugar**

¼ **cup water**

Pulp of ¼ vanilla bean

1 **large whole egg**

1 **large egg yolk**

1¾ **cups unsalted butter – room temperature**

Make a coffee extract by dissolving the instant espresso in the boiling water; set aside.

Bring the sugar, water and vanilla bean pulp to a boil in a small saucepan; stir just until the sugar dissolves. Continue to cook without stirring until the syrup reaches 255°F, as measured on a candy or instant-read thermometer. Pull the pan from the heat.

While the sugar is heating, put the egg and the yolk in the bowl of a mixer fitted with the whisk attachment and beat until the eggs are pale and foamy. When the sugar is at temperature, reduce the mixer speed to low and slowly pour in the syrup. Inevitably, some syrup will spin onto the sides of the bowl — don't try to stir the spatters into the eggs. Raise the speed to medium-high and continue to beat until the eggs are thick, satiny and room temperature, about 5 minutes.

Working with a rubber spatula, beat the butter until it is soft and creamy but not oily. With the mixer on medium speed, steadily add the butter in 2 tbsp at a time. When all the butter has been added, raise the speed to high and beat until the buttercream is thickened and satiny. Beat in the coffee extract. Chill the buttercream, stirring frequently, until it is firm enough to be spread and stay where it is spread when topped with a layer of cake, about 20 minutes. (The buttercream can be packed airtight and refrigerated for 4 days or frozen for 1 month; before using, bring it to room temperature, then beat to smooth it.)

CHOCOLATE GLAZE

5 **oz bittersweet chocolate – finely chopped**

1 **cup unsalted butter**

Bring the butter to a boil in a small saucepan. Remove the pan from the heat and clarify the butter by spooning off the top foam and pouring the clear yellow butter into a small bowl; discard the milky residue. Melt the chocolate in a bowl over— not touching—simmering water, then stir in the clarified butter.

Rum-Soaked Lemon Pound Cake

CARAMELIZED APPLES, VANILLA ICE CREAM, FROSTED PECANS, CARAMEL SAUCE

The Annapolis Valley is famous for its fruit and it extends all the way to Digby. Bruce at Ridgeview Farms has been supplying us fresh crisp apples for years delivered right to the back door.

ASSEMBLE THE PLATE

Slice the pound cake into 3 inch long fingers. Immerse three fingers of pound cake in the rum syrup for 5 - 10 second. On the plate, arrange the fingers in a triangle. Deposit a scoop of the vanilla ice cream into the center of the pound cake. Spoon some of the caramelized apples over and around the ice cream and drizzle with the caramel sauce. Garnish with some of the frosted pecans.

CARAMELIZED APPLES

- 3 tbsp unsalted butter
- 5 Honey Crisp apples – peeled, cored and cut in ½ inch wedges
- 3 tbsp brown sugar
- ½ tsp ground cinnamon
- ¼ tsp lemon zest
- ½ cup apple cider

Melt the butter in a large skillet over medium heat. Add the apples to the pan and sprinkle with 1 tbsp sugar. Sauté the apples, frequently stirring, for 6 to 8 minutes until they just begin to turn tender. Be careful not to overcook, or the apples will begin to fail and become an apple purée instead.

Sprinkle the apples with the remaining sugar, cinnamon and lemon zest. Toss the mixture gently and cook over medium heat for an additional 2 minutes until the sugar begins to caramelize, and the apples are crisp-tender.

Transfer the apples from the skillet to a serving bowl with a slotted spoon. Turn the heat up to high and add the apple cider to the skillet, scraping up any browned bits. Reduce the heat slightly and allow the cider and the pan juices to simmer for 1 to 3 minutes until the sauce has reduced and thickened slightly. Pour the finished sauce over the warm apples and serve immediately.

POUND CAKE

- 1 lb unsalted butter – softened
- 3 cups sugar
- 6 large eggs
- 4 cups all-purpose flour
- ¾ cup milk
- 1 tsp almond extract
- 1 tsp vanilla extract

Beat butter at medium speed with an electric mixer until creamy. (The butter will become a lighter yellow color; this is an important step, as the job of the mixer is to incorporate air into the butter so the cake will rise. It will take 1 to 7 minutes, depending on the power of your mixer.) Gradually add sugar, beating at medium speed until light and fluffy. (Again, the times will vary, and butter will turn to a fluffy white.) Add eggs, 1 at a time, beating just until yellow yolk disappears.

Add flour to creamed mixture alternately with milk, beginning and ending with flour. Beat at low speed just until blended after each addition. (The batter should be smooth and bits of flour should be well incorporated; to rid batter of lumps, stir gently with a rubber spatula.) Stir in extracts.

Pour into a 10 inch loaf pan. Spray the pan liberally with non-stick spray before adding the batter.

Bake at 300°F for 1 hour and 40 minutes or until a long wooden pick inserted in center comes out clean. Cool in pan on a wire rack 10 to 15 minutes. Remove from pan, and cool completely on a wire rack.

RUM SYRUP

- 2 cups water
- ½ cup dark rum
- 1 cup sugar

Bring the water, rum and sugar to a boil to dissolve the sugar. Remove from heat and cool.

VANILLA ICE CREAM

- 1½ cups 35% cream
- 1 cup whole milk
- ¼ cup sugar
- pinch of Kosher salt
- ½ vanilla bean, or 1 tsp vanilla extract
- 5 large egg yolks
- ¼ cup sugar

Combine 1½ cups heavy cream, 1 cup whole milk, ¼ cup sugar, and a pinch of kosher salt in a medium saucepan. Split ½ vanilla bean lengthwise and scrape in seeds; add pod (or use 1 tsp vanilla extract). Bring mixture just to a simmer, stirring to dissolve sugar. Remove from heat. If using vanilla bean, cover; let sit 30 minutes. Whisk 5 large egg yolks and ¼ cup sugar in a medium bowl until pale, about 2 minutes. Gradually whisk in ½ cup warm cream mixture. Whisk yolk mixture into remaining cream mixture. Cook over medium heat, stirring constantly, until thick enough to coat a wooden spoon, 2 to 3 minutes. Strain custard into a medium bowl set over a bowl of ice water; let cool, stirring occasionally. Process custard in an ice cream maker according to manufacturer's instructions. Transfer to an airtight container; cover. Freeze until firm, at least 4 hours and up to 1 week.

FROSTED PECANS

- 1 egg whites
- 2 cups pecan halves
- ½ tsp cinnamon
- 1 tsp icing sugar

Preheat oven to 250°F.

Whisk the egg whites to a broken bubbly froth. Add the walnuts, cinnamon and icing sugar. Bake in the oven for 1 hour, turning after 30 minutes. Cool and serve.

TIP: Pecans will be soft immediately from the oven, but will crisp as they cool

CARAMEL SAUCE

- 1 cup granulated sugar
- ¼ cup water
- 10 tbsp 35% cream
- 5 tbsp unsalted butter – cut into cubes

In a medium heavy bottom saucepan heat the water and sugar over medium-low heat. Whisk constantly until the sugar has dissolved and the mixture starts to just bubble.

Turn the heat to high and bring to a boil. Stop stirring and allow mixture to continue boiling until it turns amber color. This could take 8 to 12 minutes.

Remove from the heat and carefully and slowly whisk in the heavy cream as the mixture will bubble. Mix in the butter, one cube at a time until everything is incorporated.

Turn off the heat and allow the mixture to cool in the pot for 10 to 15 minutes stirring occasionally. The mixture will thicken as it cools.

Nova Scotia Blueberry 'Misu'

SAVOIARDI COOKIES SOAKED IN BLUEBERRY JUICE AND
COGNAC, WHIPPED MASCARPONE, BLUEBERRY COMPOTE,
CARAMEL, SHAVED CHOCOLATE

The Italian classic dessert with an Oxford, NS blueberry twist.
Blueberry juice and Grand Marnier in place of the espresso marsala
and lots of blueberry compote and fresh local blueberries.

Serves 4

DIGBY PINES BLUEBERRY COMPOTE

- 4 cups frozen blueberries
- 1 tsp cinnamon
- ½ tsp allspice
- 1 tbsp brown sugar
  Juice of one lemon
- 1 tbsp cornstarch
- ¼ cup water

Put all ingredients in a medium sized saucepan. Bring to a boil and simmer until thick.

CARAMEL SAUCE

- 1 cup granulated sugar
- ¼ cup water
- 10 tbsp 35% cream
- 5 tbsp unsalted butter – cut into cubes

In a medium heavy bottom saucepan heat the water and sugar over medium-low heat. Whisk constantly until the sugar has dissolved and the mixture starts to just bubble.

Turn the heat to high and bring to a boil. Stop stirring and allow mixture to continue boiling until it turns amber color. This could take 8 to 12 minutes.

Remove from the heat and carefully and slowly whisk in the heavy cream as the mixture will bubble. Mix in the butter, one cube at a time until everything is incorporated.

Turn off the heat and allow the mixture to cool in the pot for 10 to 15 minutes stirring occasionally. The mixture will thicken as it cools.

WHIPPED MASCARPONE

- 6 large egg yolks
- 1 cup sugar
- 1¼ cup mascarpone cheese
- 1¾ cup 35% cream

Combine egg yolks and sugar in the top of a double boiler. Reduce heat to low, and cook for about 10 minutes, stirring constantly. This is your sabayon, remove from the heat and whip yolks until thick and lemon-colored. Allow to cool briefly before mixing in mascarpone. Add mascarpone to whipped yolks, beat until combined.

In a separate bowl, whip cream to stiff peaks. Gently fold the whipped cream in the mascarpone sabayon mixture and set aside. The mascarpone does not have to be at room temperature, but it will help it mix in easier if it is. Take it out of the refrigerator as you gather ingredients to make the recipe.

ASSEMBLE THE MISU

- 2 7 oz packages Italian lady fingers
- 1 cup POM blueberry juice
- 2 oz cognac

In four martini glasses, spoon a small amount of the mascarpone in the bottom of each glass. Soak one lady finger in the POM cognac syrup, break in half and put on top of the mascarpone. Spoon a bit of blueberry compote over the lady finger. Repeat with more mascarpone, another lady finger and compote. Finish with the rest of the mascarpone and smooth the surface. Drizzle the top with caramel sauce and some of the leftover blueberry compote.

TIP: An attractive garnish is a rosette of whipped cream and shaved chocolate

Lemon Cheesecake with Summer Berry Compote

SWEET PASTRY CRUST, BLACKBERRY PURÉE

Cheesecake is always a popular dessert. Add the lemon buzz word and it doesn't stay in the fridge. The berries can change, or serve it with other sauces if you wish, but it will always be delicious.

Serves 8

FILLING

- ¼ cup fresh lemon juice
- 1 pkg unflavoured gelatin
- 2 cups cream cheese
- 1 cup vanilla Greek yogurt
  Zest of one lemon
- 1 tsp vanilla extract
- 1¼ cup icing sugar
- 1 cup 35% cream

In a small bowl, sprinkle the gelatin evenly over the lemon juice. Let stand for 1 minute. Microwave on high for 20 to 30 seconds until hot and whisk until dissolved. Set aside to cool to room temperature.

In a large bowl, beat the cream cheese until fluffy. Add the Greek yogurt and beat until combined.

Add the gelatin mixture, lemon zest, vanilla and sugar and beat until combined.

Add whipping cream and beat on low until combined, then beat on high for 3 to 5 minutes until fluffy and thickened, (the mixture should hold stiff peaks on the beaters).

POUR FILLING INTO PREPARED MOLDS:
Use 2 inch ring molds that stand 2½ inches high. Line the inside of the mold with parchment or acetate tape. Place one of the sweet pastry discs at the bottom of the mold. Using a piping bag, pipe the cheesecake filling so that it is level with the top of the mold. Refrigerate 5 to 6 hours or until firmly set.

Unmold the cheesecake and place it on a plate. Place a few fresh berries on top of the cheesecake. Spoon a small pile of the summer berry compote near the base, and drag some of the blackberry purée around the plate.

SWEET PASTRY CRUST

- 1½ cups all-purpose flour
- ⅛ tsp salt
- ½ cup unsalted butter –
  room temperature
- ¼ cup granulated white sugar
- 1 large egg – lightly beaten

Preheat oven to 350°F

In a separate bowl, whisk the flour with the salt. Place the butter in the bowl of your electric mixer, or with a hand mixer, and beat until softened. Add sugar and beat until light and fluffy. Gradually add the beaten egg, beating just until incorporated. Add the flour mixture all at once and mix until it forms a ball. Flatten the pastry into a disk, cover with plastic wrap, and refrigerate for 15 to 30 minutes or until firm.

Once the pastry has chilled sufficiently, roll the pastry out to a thickness of ¼ inch thick. Using a 2 inch cookie cutter, cut as many sweet pastry rounds as possible.

Place the pastry rounds on parchment paper and lightly prick them with the tines of a fork. Bake the sweet pastry rounds in the oven for about 15 minutes. Remove from the oven and place on a wire rack to cool.

SUMMER BERRY COMPOTE

- ½ cup frozen blueberries
- ½ cup frozen blackberries
- 1 cup fresh raspberries
- 1 cup fresh strawberries
- 1 tsp cinnamon
- ¼ tsp allspice
- 2 tbsp brown sugar
  Juice of one lemon
- 1 tbsp cornstarch
- ½ cup water

Put all ingredients in a medium sized saucepan. Bring to a boil and simmer until thick.

BLACKBERRY PURÉE

- 2 cups frozen blackberries
- ½ cup icing sugar
  Juice from ½ lemon

Put all of the ingredients into a blender and purée until smooth. Strain through a sieve and hold in the refrigerator.

Belgian Flourless Chocolate Truffle Cake

COFFEE ICE CREAM, FRESH RASPBERRIES, APRICOT DRIZZLE

I have been making this cake for most of my professional career. It is a delicate process, and the folding of the egg into the chocolate is key for a lighter aerated result. Either way, you will have chocolatey decadent cake to satisfy your cravings.

Makes one 10 inch round cake

1 **lb Belgian chocolate – cut in small pieces**
¼ **cup butter**
10 **whole eggs**
¾ **cup sugar**

Preheat oven to 250°F.

Prepare a 10 inch spring form pan. Spray the side and bottom with non-stick spray and line the bottom with parchment paper that is slightly larger than the bottom of the pan.

Melt the chocolate and butter together in a stainless-steel bowl over a water bath, stirring occasionally with a rubber spatula. Set aside.

In a stainless-steel bowl, combine the eggs and sugar. Whisk the eggs and sugar until they triple in volume and cook to a firm ribbon. This may take 10 minutes of continuous whisking to achieve a firm "figure 8" ribbon.

Cool each mixture to 96°F.

In three stages, carefully fold the egg/sugar mixture into the chocolate mixture. The first stage introduces the eggs to the chocolate and begins the process. The second stage will begin to build volume for your cake, and the third stage will complete the light chocolaty batter. It is important not to overwork the mixture and lose the volume of air from the cake.

Pour the batter into the spring form pan and smooth evenly with a spatula. Bake for one hour in the center of the oven until the middle of the cake is set firm. Allow to cool before removing from the pan to cut.

COFFEE ICE CREAM
makes 4 cups

1½ **cups whole milk**
¾ **cup sugar**
1½ **cups whole coffee beans**
    Pinch of salt
1½ **cups heavy cream**
5 **large egg yolks**
¼ **tsp vanilla extract**
¼ **tsp finely ground coffee**

Heat the milk, sugar, whole coffee beans, salt, and ½ cup of the cream in a medium saucepan until warm but not boiling. Once the mixture is warm, cover, remove from the heat, and let steep at room temperature for 1 hour.

Pour the remaining 1 cup of cream into a medium size metal bowl, set on ice over a larger bowl. Set a mesh strainer on top of the bowls. Set aside.

Reheat the milk and coffee mixture. In a separate bowl, whisk the egg yolks together. Slowly pour the heated milk and coffee mixture into the egg yolks, whisking constantly so that the egg yolks are tempered by the warm milk. Scrape the warmed egg yolks back into the saucepan.

Stir the mixture constantly over medium heat with a heatproof, flat-bottomed spatula, scraping the bottom as you stir, until the mixture thickens and coats the spatula so that you can run your finger across the coating leaving a clean line. This can take about 10 minutes.

Pour the custard through the strainer and stir it into the cream. Press on the coffee beans in the strainer to extract as much of the coffee flavor as possible. Discard the beans. Mix in the vanilla and finely ground coffee, and stir until cool.

Chill the mixture thoroughly in the refrigerator, then freeze it in your ice cream maker according to the manufacturer's instructions.

APRICOT DRIZZLE

makes 1 cup

1¼ **cups apricot preserves**

2 **tbsp golden rum**

4 **tbsp water**

Bring the preserves and rum to a boil in a small saucepan over medium heat, stirring often. Cook until the apricot coats the back of a spoon 4 to 5 minutes. Strain through a wire sieve into a small bowl, pressing hard on the solids.

Chill glaze and refrigerate.

Bumbleberry Shortcake

SHORTCAKE BISCUIT, STRAWBERRY RASPBERRY COULIS,
CHANTILLY CREAM

Berry Shortcake is still a significant comfort food dessert and is the number one dessert requested by our banquet clients. It pleases everybody, and if it is prepared with care, it is a light tasty finish to a great meal.

SHORTCAKE BISCUIT

- 2 cups all-purpose flour
- 1 tbsp baking powder
- ½ tsp salt
- 3 tbsp sugar
- ¼ lb butter – chilled
- ¾ cup 18% cream

Preheat the oven to 425°F.

In large bowl combine the flour, baking powder, salt, and 3 tbsp of sugar. Blend well. Slice the butter into 8 pieces and add to the mixture. Blend with a pastry cutter or fingertips until the mixture resembles coarse meal. Make a well in the center. With a fork, stir in the cream just until the dough is moist. Be very careful not to overwork the dough. Let the dough rest for a minute.

Turn the dough out onto a lightly floured surface. Fold the dough over on itself 2 or 3 times, until it is holding together and is less sticky. Gently pat the dough into a 6 × 12 inch rectangle about ¾ inch thick and cut 8 (3 inch) biscuits with a floured cutter.

Arrange the biscuits on a prepared baking sheet. Brush the biscuits with some cream and sprinkle tops with some sugar.

Bake the biscuits in the preheated oven for 10 to 15 minutes, until risen and golden brown.

CHANTILLY WHIPPED CREAM

- 2 cups 35% cream
- ½ cup sugar
- 1 tsp vanilla extract
-   Zest from one lemon

Using a mixer, beat the heavy cream, sugar, vanilla, and lemon zest until soft peaks form, about 1½ to 2 minutes.

STRAWBERRY RASPBERRY COULIS

- 1 cup frozen strawberries – thawed
- 1 cup frozen raspberries – thawed
- 4 tbsp icing sugar

Combine the berries and icing sugar in a blender and purée until smooth. Strain out the seeds.

BUMBLEBERRY COMPOTE

- 1½ lbs mixture of strawberries (stemmed and quartered), blueberries, blackberries and raspberries
- ½ cup icing sugar
-   Juice from 1 lemon
- 1 tbsp cornstarch

Combine all ingredients in a small saucepan and bring to a boil. Turn heat to medium low, stir occasionally until the compote thickens. Chill for later use.

RECIPE APPENDIX

SAUCES

MINNIE AND BO WAFFORD BBQ SAUCE

Makes 1 quart

- 2 tbsp butter
- 1 medium onion – peeled and finely chopped
- 1 tsp garlic – minced
- ½ cup dark brown sugar
- ¼ tsp ground black pepper
- ½ tsp salt
- 1½ tbsp Dijon mustard
- 1 tbsp cider vinegar
- 1 tbsp fresh lemon juice
- 3 tbsp Worcestershire sauce
- 2 cups ketchup
- 2 cups water

Heat the butter in a saucepan, and when hot, add the onion and garlic. Saute over medium heat for 5 minutes, until the onion is translucent, then add the brown sugar, pepper, salt, and mustard. Stir constantly over low heat for 2 minutes, then add the remaining ingredients.

Bring to a boil over medium heat and simmer, stirring occasionally, for 25 to 30 minutes.

TIP: The sauce can be stored in the refrigerator in jars with tight fitting lids for up to 3 months.

BASIL CREAM SAUCE

- 1 tbsp butter
- 1 garlic clove – chopped fine
- ½ cup white wine
- 2 cups 35% cream
- ¼ tsp salt
- ½ cup fresh basil – chopped, or use 1 tbsp dried basil
- ¼ cup parmesan cheese – grated
  Black pepper – to taste

Melt the butter in sauce pan and saute garlic for 1 minute. Add the white wine and reduce to about ¼ cup. Add the heavy cream and bring to a boil and reduce slightly. Season with salt and pepper, add the fresh basil and the parmesan cheese. Stir well to melt cheese and blend flavours.

LEMON BUTTER SAUCE

- ⅔ cup white wine
- 1½ tsp shallots, chopped
- 1 tbsp lemon juice – freshly squeezed
- ⅔ cup 35% cream
- 1 cup unsalted butter
  Salt and pepper to taste

In a saucepan over medium heat, add wine, shallots and lemon juice and reduce volume by half. Add the cream and reduce for another five minutes. Cut the butter into cubes and add slowly to the cream mixture over medium heat, whisking until a smooth sauce is obtained. Season to taste.

CRÈME ANGLAISE

- 2 cups 35% cream
- ½ vanilla bean – split lengthwise, seed removed
- 4 egg yolks
- ⅓ cup sugar

In a saucepan, combine the cream with the vanilla bean and bring to a boil.

In a heat proof bowl, beat together the yolks with the sugar until smooth.

Pour the cream into the yolk mixture and beat together.

Pour the mixture back into the saucepan and heat slowly, stirring constantly. When the mixture thickens enough to coat the back of a spoon. Remove from the heat, remove the vanilla bean (save, packed in sugar for later use) and cool over an ice bath stirring occasionally until cold.

DRESSINGS / CONDIMENTS

MANGO CHIPOTLE CATSUP

- 2 tbsp vegetable oil
- 1 red onion – diced small
- 3 ripe mangoes – peeled, pitted, and cut in bite-size chunks
- ½ cup packed brown sugar
- ½ cup red wine vinegar
- 2 or 3 canned chipotle peppers
- ¼ cup molasses
  Salt and fresh cracked black pepper to taste

In a large saucepan, heat the oil over medium heat until hot but not smoking. Add the onion and cook, stirring occasionally, until well browned, 7 to 9 minutes.

Add the mangoes, brown sugar, vinegar, chipotle peppers, and molasses. Bring to a boil, reduce the heat to low, and simmer, stirring occasionally, until well thickened, about 1 hour. Be careful not to burn.

Remove the mixture from the heat, allow to cool somewhat, then purée in a food processor or blender. Season with salt and pepper.

Will keep, covered and refrigerated, for about 2 weeks.

LEMON GARLIC AIOLI

- 2 tbsp roasted garlic
- 1 tbsp white wine vinegar
- 1 tbsp lemon juice
- 2 large egg yolks
- ½ cup extra virgin olive oil
- ½ cup canola oil
- Kosher salt and black pepper

In a blender or food processor, combine the garlic, vinegar, lemon juice and egg yolks. Blend on high speed. Slowly drizzle in the olive and canola oils to form an emulsion. If the mixture becomes too thick, add a splash of water to achieve the correct consistency. Season with kosher salt and pepper.

PICKLED NAPA CABBAGE SLAW

- ½ cup rice vinegar
- ¼ cup plus 2 tbsp sugar
- 1 tbsp ginger – finely chopped
- 2 tsp salt
- ½ tsp garlic – finely chopped
- 3 whole cloves
- 5 medium carrots – cut in 3 × ⅛ inch julienne
- ¾ lb snow peas – cut in julienne
- 1¼ lb Napa cabbage – leaves halved lengthwise, then cut crosswise into ¼ inch strips
- 2 tbsp jalapeno pepper – seeded and thinly sliced julienne

Bring vinegar, sugar, ginger, salt, garlic, and cloves to a boil in a small saucepan, stirring until sugar is dissolved, then remove from heat and let steep, uncovered, 30 minutes. Discard cloves.

While pickling liquid steeps, blanch carrots in a 6- to 8-quart pot of boiling salted water 30 seconds, then transfer with a large slotted spoon to a bowl of ice and cold water to stop cooking. Lift out carrots with slotted spoon and drain in a colander. Transfer to paper towels and pat dry.

Blanch snow peas in same pot of boiling water 30 seconds, then transfer to ice water, drain, and pat dry in same manner. Cut each snow pea lengthwise into 4 strips.

Blanch cabbage in same pot of boiling water 5 seconds, then transfer to ice water, drain, and pat dry.

Just before serving, toss vegetables with pickling liquid and jalapeno in a large bowl.

CHERRY APPLE ALMOND CHUTNEY

- 1 oz canola oil
- 1 medium onion – diced
- 2 cups Gala apples – cored and chopped in ½ inch cubes
- 1 cup canned cherries – use fresh pitted if you prefer
- 1 cup apple juice
- ¼ cup brown sugar
- ½ cup apple cider vinegar
- ¾ cup almond sticks – toasted
- ¼ cup chopped parsley

In a medium saucepan, saute the onion in canola oil for 5 to 6 minutes. Add in the apples, cherries, apple juice, brown sugar and cider vinegar. Bring to a boil and reduce the heat to simmer. Cook the chutney until it begins to thicken from the apple pectin, cherries breaking down and the sugar reducing. When it looks thick enough after about 20 minutes, add in the almond sticks and chopped parsley.

GRILLED STONEFRUIT CHUTNEY

- 2 tbsp vegetable oil
- 1 large yellow onion – cut in julienne
- 4 apricots
- 4 red plums
- 2 nectarines
- 2 peaches
- ½ cup packed brown sugar
- ¼ cup white sugar
- 2 tbsp molasses
- ½ cup golden raisins
- 1 tsp salt
- 1 tsp fresh cracked white pepper
- 1 tsp crushed star anise
- Pinch ground mace
- ½ cup red wine vinegar
- ¼ cup white vinegar
- 2 tbsp lemon juice

Turn on the BBQ to medium-high heat.

Cut the fruit in half. Remove the stones from the middle and put the fruit in a separate bowl. Add a little canola oil and season with a little salt and pepper. Lay the fruit all over the BBQ and mark well but do not burn. Return to the bowl and chill. Cut the stone fruit into ½ inch cubes.

Heat the oil in a large saucepan over medium heat until hot but not smoking.

Add the onions and saute until translucent, 5 to 7 minutes.

Add the grilled stone fruit and cook, stirring frequently, for 4 minutes.

Add all the remaining ingredients except ¼ cup of white vinegar and lemon juice.

Turn the heat to low and simmer, uncovered, for one hour, stirring occasionally. Watch to be sure the mixture does not burn.

Remove from heat, add the remaining vinegar and the lemon juice, and mix thoroughly.

Serve at room temperature. The chutney will keep, covered and refrigerated for several weeks.

Edible flowers from the Pines' herb garden

SWEET N' SOUR RHUBARB CHUTNEY

- 1 lb rhubarb – cut in 1½ inch long by ¼ × ¼ inch thick baton
- 5 tbsp apple cider vinegar
- 5 tbsp granulated sugar
- 3 tbsp water

Heat the vinegar, sugar and water until the sugar dissolves.

Add the rhubarb, cover and cook for about 20 seconds.

Remove the rhubarb to a bowl and reduce the sugar syrup to about 5 tbsp.

Pour the syrup over the rhubarb and cool.

SPICED APPLES

- 2 tsp olive oil
- 2 braising apples (preferably Fuji) – peeled and cut into ¼ inch dice
- 1 star anise
- 3 whole cloves
- ½ stick cinnamon
- Pinch of salt
- 2 tbsp brown sugar
- ¼ cup Riesling or other sweet wine

Heat a small saucepan on medium-high and add the olive oil, apple, star anise, cloves, cinnamon, and a pinch of salt. Stir frequently to avoid excessive browning.

As soon as the apples begin to take on color, add the sugar and half the Riesling.

Reduce to thick syrup and remove from the heat and set aside to cool.

PAN JUICES
FOR 100 KILOMETRE EXPERIENCE

- 1 **lb chicken bones**
- 1 **onion – roughly chopped**
- 2 **carrots – roughly chopped**
- 2 **stalks celery – roughly chopped**
- 1 **cup white wine**
- 4 **bay leaves**
- 1 **tbsp fresh thyme – stalks and all**
- 1 **tsp black peppercorns**
- 4 **quarts water**

TIP: Buy as much locally sourced product as possible

Preheat the oven to 350°F.

In a large oven proof pan, roast the chicken bones until they begin to brown around the edges, about 30 to 45 minutes. Add the chopped vegetables and continue to roast until the bones and vegetables are well browned. This process can take about an hour.

Add in the white wine and scrape the pan to release any particles of chicken that may have adhered to the bottom.

Transfer the bones, the vegetables and all the scrapings to a large sauce pot.

Add 1 quart of water and bring to a boil. Turn the temperature to medium, allowing the water to reduce to about half its volume. Repeat this process with the remainder of the water, 1 quart at a time. With each successive water reduction, the juices with take on more and more flavor and brown color as it is extracted from the chicken bones. Reduce the final water reduction to about 2 cups. Strain the juices and hold on the side for your dinner service.

BASIC RECIPES

ROASTING GARLIC THE QUICK WAY

- 2 **whole buds garlic – separated and peeled**
- 2 **tbsp canola oil**
- 1 **cup white wine**
- **Salt and pepper**
- 4 **cups mayonnaise**

Heat the oil in a small fry pan. Add the garlic cloves and sautee until light brown. Add half the white wine, turn the heat to med low, and allow the wine to evaporate and poach the garlic. When the wine has disappeared, let the garlic fry for a few minutes to soften and caramelize to the pan. Do not burn. Repeat with the remaining white wine. Finish by letting the garlic pick up good browning in the pan to create great flavor.

Fork mash the garlic and add it to the mayonnaise.

This process will rid the garlic of the strong acidic flavor of the garlic, leaving the beautiful roasted flavor you enjoy. Garlic prepared this way has many other uses.

PINES STEAK RUB

- 8 **tbsp Montreal steak spice**
- 4 **tbsp smoked paprika**
- 4 **tbsp paprika**
- 1 **tbsp powder**
- 1 **tbsp chili powder**
- 1 **tbsp dried thyme**
- 1 **tbsp dried basil**
- 1 **tbsp dried oregano**
- ½ **cup canola oil**

Combine all the dried ingredients and mix together well. Add the canola oil and stir together. The canola oil will absorb into the spices, so you may have to add a little more oil to keep the rub spreadable.

DUCK CONFIT

- 3 **tbsp salt**
- 4 **cloves garlic – smashed**
- 1 **medium onion – sliced**
- 4 **tsp dried thyme**
- 3 **tsp black peppercorns – crushed**
- 8 **duck legs**
- 4 **cups duck fat**

Sprinkle 1 tbsp of salt in the bottom of a dish or plastic container large enough to hold the duck legs in a single layer. Evenly scatter half the garlic, onion, and thyme in the container. Arrange the duck, skin-side up, over the salt mixture, then sprinkle with the remaining salt, garlic, shallots, thyme and pepper. Cover and refrigerate for 1 to 2 days.

Preheat the oven to 225°F. Melt the duck fat in a small saucepan. Brush the salt and seasoning off the duck. Arrange the duck pieces in a single layer in a high-sided baking dish or ovenproof saucepan. Pour the melted fat over the duck (the duck pieces should be covered by fat) and place the confit in the oven. Cook the confit slowly at a very slow simmer, until the duck is tender and can be easily pulled from the bone, 6 to 8 hours. Remove the confit from the oven. Cool and store the duck in the fat.

TIP: The confit will keep in the refrigerator for several weeks

INDEX

Dale Nichols

A native of Moncton, New Brunswick, Chef Dale Nichols started his culinary career in 1981 apprenticing and working in several of Toronto's notable hot spots. He attributes his knowledge and approach to the kitchen to his mentor Mark McEwen, with whom he worked for over nine years.

In 1995, Chef Nichols and his family moved back to east coast Halifax as Executive Chef of the former Canadian Pacific Chateau Halifax (currently Delta Halifax) and established himself as a promoter and user of local products. After joining Newcastle Hotels and Resorts in 2003, Chef Nichols became Executive Chef of the Digby Pines Golf Resort and Spa in 2009 and bases a majority of his menus around locally-sourced produce and proteins.

Chef Nichols lives on property at The Pines during the busy summer months and resides in Halifax during the winter off season. He gives back to the community by making himself available to select fund raisers and charitable causes.

Philosophy: Develop a solid work ethic, leave your EGO at the door and bring your PRIDE inside.

Lynda Shalagan

Lynda Shalagan grew up in Vancouver, B.C. She began taking craft and fine art courses at Capilano College in North Vancouver and subsequently transferred to the Nova Scotia College of Art and Design, Halifax, N.S. (BFA '82). At present, Lynda lives in Halifax and continues her work in painting at her studio/Artz Gallery exhibiting locally and nationally. Her work oscillates between representation and abstraction in a continuing study of the textures, patterns and processes found in nature. See her work at www.lyndashalagan.com

Notes